Machine Learning with Dynamics 365 and Power Platform

Machine Learning with Dynamics 365 and Power Platform

The Ultimate Guide to Apply Predictive Analytics

AURELIEN CLERE

VINNIE BANSAL

WILEY

Library of Congress Cataloging-in-Publication Data

Names: Clere, Aurelien, author. | Bansal, Vinnie, author.
Title: Machine learning with Dynamics 365 and Power Platform : the ultimate guide to apply predictive analytics / Aurelien Clere, Vinnie Bansal.
Description: Hoboken, New Jersey : Wiley, [2022] | Includes index.
Identifiers: LCCN 2021040966 (print) | LCCN 2021040967 (ebook) | ISBN 9781119771296 (cloth) | ISBN 9781119771319 (adobe pdf) | ISBN 9781119771302 (epub)
Subjects: LCSH: Microsoft Corporation. | Machine learning.
Classification: LCC Q325.5 .C54 2022 (print) | LCC Q325.5 (ebook) | DDC 006.3/1—dc23
LC record available at https://lccn.loc.gov/2021040966
LC ebook record available at https://lccn.loc.gov/2021040967

Cover Design: Wiley
Cover Image: © Immersion Imagery/Shutterstock

SKY10031566_112221

Contents

Foreword

Y OU MIGHT BE WONDERING what machine learning and artificial intelligence (ML/AI) along with Microsoft Dynamics 365 and the Microsoft Power Platform have in common or even what they have to do with each other. But I might challenge you to think bigger and ask not what they have to do with each other; rather, ask how they can work together.

It is not enough these days to just implement your enterprise resource planning (ERP) or customer relationship management (CRM) system and walk away. Sure, you can optimize and improve business processes with a new system, but if you really want to digitally transform and reduce your operating costs to see the full return on investment, then you will need to look beyond just moving your basic business processes into a new system. This is where ML/AI can come into play.

Most organizations don't choose to replace their ERP system for the sake of replacement. Instead, ERP systems are replaced by necessity and a culmination of events and circumstances that usually *require* a system to be replaced. Replacing an ERP is a difficult and time-consuming process in and of itself, but you would be remiss to not consider how you can leverage emerging technologies such as ML/AI in this process to get more value out of your investment. Whether you are considering a new ERP, or you have been running Dynamics 365 for some time, this book offers practical advice for leveraging ML/AI to achieve more with your solution.

There are tons of books out there that can give you all the technical and mathematical theory that goes along with ML/AI, but this book is the first to bring real-life examples and experiences that show you how to apply ML/AI to your Dynamics 365 and Power Platform projects.

In my 12-part TechTalk series on using the Power Platform to extend Dynamics 365 Finance and Operations apps, one key message throughout is about using the technologies together to bring more value at a faster pace. The authors of this book capture this essence and take it three steps further by giving you all the details you need to be successful in making your solution come to life with Dynamics 365, the Power Platform, and ML/AI.

What I like about this book is that the authors really showcase their expertise. They provide not only real-life examples to help you relate to your business, but they also provide the details and technical advice required to achieve similar results in your own organization. I can recall the first time I worked with Aurelien to co-present at a virtual conference on the topic of virtual entities with Finance and Operations apps. His passion for adopting and using hot new technology was evident. The passion shown by Aurelien and Vinnie for helping the community with their knowledge and expertise has always been evident, and this book is just another great example. I believe that when you combine the passion for the technology with the passion for the community, the reader can only benefit from the knowledge and experience of the authors.

I recommend that you read this insightful book, full of practical advice and technical guidance no matter where you are in your Dynamics 365 implementation to help shape your digital transformation.

Rachel Profitt
Senior Program Manager, Microsoft

Preface

WITH MACHINE LEARNING AND artificial intelligence contributing solutions to many sectors from communication and finance to transportation, manufacturing, and even agriculture, enterprises are accelerating their adoption of AI, focusing on those initiatives that can help them achieve revenue growth and cost reduction. In this book, we want to show you how the fusion of the two technologies, Machine Learning and Dynamics 365, can help you to build solutions that can solve real-world problems. With the knowledge in this book, you can build your own system that can help you make more efficient and intelligent business decisions. There are tons of ML applications in the market today, and the learning is endless; and, considering the intensity with which the data is growing, it's only wise to use this data to make intelligent systems for your business. This book is your companion to machine learning with Dynamics 365 and Power Platform. Whether you are a Dynamics 365 and Power Platform developer or a technical consultant or solution architect new to machine learning or someone who wants to deepen your knowledge of the latest developments, this book is the one stop.

WHY DID WE WRITE THIS BOOK?

In the current market, not many books offer information on incorporating machine learning in Dynamics 365 and Power Platform or provide any practical examples. This is the first book focusing on machine learning with Microsoft Dynamics 365 and Power Platform that provides tips and techniques for organizations that are planning their digital transformation journey.

The book is a practical approach to understanding the concepts of machine learning and deep learning.

WHAT WAS THE INSPIRATION BEHIND THIS SUBJECT?

The truth is that developers, technical consultants, and solution architects are constantly being assessed on their knowledge and skills. So how can they stay on top of the game?

Goalposts in the workplace and/or projects keep moving. This might be because of new technologies such as artificial intelligence/machine learning (AI/ML), customer demand, or simply because there is a new program director with a different vision. All these changes invariably have implications for us. So, if you want to protect your employability, you need to take charge of your personal development.

No doubt machine learning is a highly trending technology these days for different kinds of business applications and is one of the hottest topics in AI. When combined with Microsoft Dynamics 365 and Power Platform, it can do wonders for its users, which includes getting experimental results and deriving conclusions by utilizing the past data. A blend of machine learning and Microsoft Business Applications Solutions Ecosystem (BASE) and/or Dynamics 365 and Power Platform is beneficial for businesses to make proactive decisions by using predictive data analytics. It also provides businesses the ability to utilize future predictions in order to perform operations more efficiently.

Acknowledgments

W HETHER WATCHING AN AWARD-WINNING movie in a cinema hall or having the luxury of watching from home in recent times, the audience is left with a lasting impression by the actors. Usually, the actors and directors are awarded, but there is much more to it than meets the eye. There is a huge team of people that supports and contributes to making a movie a success. Until we wrote this book, we didn't realize the amount of effort that goes into the making of a book. We are profoundly grateful for our incredibly supportive, respected, and diligent advisory team who made this dream possible. This book is theirs as much as ours.

The initial drafts of the book have passed multiple hands and undergone several revisions. Each revision provided us with invaluable feedback from the following reviewers. They have been relentless in their contributions, which enabled us to include additional concepts, refine ideas, increase our focus, add clarity, and continuously evolve.

We owe immense gratitude to all our reviewers, who are industry experts and leaders in their own professions and gave their time by providing great input and valuable suggestions, offering insights, and challenging the draft chapters constructively throughout the production of the book. Without their support our work would not have evolved into the book that you are reading now.

We are forever indebted to all of them:

Saurabh Nijhawan—Lead Consultant at Microsoft

Nick Brady—Senior Program Manager at Microsoft

Stefaan Lampaert—Enterprise Solution Architect at Microsoft

Fredrik Saetre—Technology Specialist Manager at Microsoft

Deepak Agarwal—Project Lead at KPMG, Microsoft MVP

Christopher Davis—Technical Strategist at Microsoft

Vadim Korepin—Functional Architect at Microsoft

Markus Turunen—CIO and Business Lead (Machine Learning and Intelligent Automation)

Monika Adams—D365 CE Enthusiast

Manali Tiwari—Technical Writer

Sneh Swaroop—Technical Consultant at Microsoft

Rajkiran Divekar—IT Manager

Fawad Khan—Digital Community and Social Leader for Dynamics 365 at Microsoft

Manish Rajput—AI/ML Practitioner

May Alhajri—Digital Analyst, Microsoft MVP

Anupama Natarajan—Data & AI Consultant, MCT, Microsoft AI MVP

About the Authors

AURELIEN CLERE was a Global Technical Architect in the Microsoft Business Application ecosystem for more than 12 years. Aurelien is a Microsoft Most Valuable Professional (MVP) and Microsoft Certified Trainer (MCT) with more than 15 Microsoft certifications. He started his career in Microsoft Business Applications with Dynamics AX and Dynamics CRM. Following the strategy of pushing his knowledge to have a global overview on Microsoft applications, he joined the Azure side in 2013 with a French start-up to develop an ISV with Dynamics CRM and all Azure components (Data Platform, Machine Learning).

Aurelien is now working for a French Dynamics Partner called Dynagile Consulting. He's been working for several years on the Architecture side with the conception, integration, and deployment of Dynamics 365 Finance Operations, Power Platform, Dynamics 365 CE, and Azure components (Azure Data Lake, Azure Synapse Analytics, and Azure Machine Learning).

He is also known for organizing the Power Platform French Summit with more than 2,000 participants. With his blog (powerazure365.com) and his YouTube channel, and all his sessions in community events, he shares his knowledge to help with leveraging data in Dynamics 365.

His main focuses are:

Dynamics 365 Finance and Operations
Dynamics 365 AI: Customer Insights with Azure Machine Learning, Finance Insights

AI: All Azure Cognitive Services, Azure ML, AI Builder, Bot Service with PVA

Power Platform (PowerBI, Power Apps and Power Automate, PVA)

Azure Data Lake with Dynamics 365

Data Insights / ML Insights / Predictions / AI Builder in Dynamics365 projects with Azure components + Azure AI Services

Data Platform: Azure Synapse Analytics with Data Lake of Dynamics 365 Data – Azure Purview and PowerBI – Modern Data warehouse

VINNIE BANSAL has passion and expertise for envisioning the big picture by working with the customers of Dynamics 365 Finance and Dynamics 365 Supply Chain Management to assist the innovation process, end-to-end, and to empower enterprises to overcome their biggest hurdles, streamline complex "pain points," realize their goals, and achieve business transformation.

His deep understanding of the Microsoft Dynamics 365 application and his exceptional professional relations skills have made him a valuable contributor to every customer he has had the privilege to support over the past 14 years.

Realization of functional fit/gap analysis takes on an active functional role during the discovery and implementation process: analyzing and optimizing business processes in order to provide the best functional and/or technical solutions; providing multiple solutions to a problem; and at the same time evaluating the business impact of the solutions.

To give back to the Microsoft Dynamics 365 community and industry, he regularly shares his experiences, customer solutions, and learning in his LinkedIn posts and articles. He believes in staying updated with industry best practices and keeping himself with the best in the domain.

CHAPTER ONE

Dynamics 365, Power Platform, and Machine Learning

 INTRODUCTION TO DYNAMICS 365

There was a time when businesses used individual applications to perform several business functions like marketing, field service, project service, customer service, operations, and finance. No one ever imagined how difficult and time-consuming it would be to navigate from

For digital transformation to happen, we needed an intelligent system that can be molded to all businesses and has the agility to evolve and expand as the business changes. Such a system can consolidate individual apps that you use for customer service, sales, or field service; can be easily deployed and customized; and, most of all, can provide a unified experience.

one application to another and maintain large amounts of data that were growing every second.

Here comes Microsoft Dynamics 365. It is a set of cloud-based business applications, such as components of customer relationship management (CRM) and enterprise resource planning (ERP), along with productive applications and artificial intelligence tools, all together in one platform. Dynamics 365 brought an end to information silos between the CRM and ERP, all because of a shared business database known as the Common Data Model, which helps you to overcome obstacles between critical business platforms and make your data work together.

Microsoft Business Applications

Who doesn't want to envision the future of their business? And what's better than relying on customers for the transformation of your business? Understanding what customers want is one of the biggest challenges faced by businesses today. To understand what customers want requires focusing on these four transformational outcomes:

1. **Empowering employees.** Dynamics 365 empowers employees by giving them tools and actionable insights with the knowledge and information required to operate in real time.
2. **Engaging customers.** Dynamics 365 improves customer engagement by enabling employees to connect with potential customers proactively and regularly capture customer feedback to provide a personalized service experience.
3. **Optimizing operations.** Dynamics 365 provides a central source of intelligence that offers instant knowledge of your global workforce and supply chain with the flexibility to collaborate with various devices anytime to manage operations effectively and build innovative products.
4. **Modifying the products or services in the business model.** Dynamics 365 streamlines all your business processes and analyzes your business requirements to help you achieve your desired goal.

These four areas give an organization a comprehensive view to provide a standard rich data model that can consistently work across all your business applications to connect customers, products, people, and data.

Customer Relationship Management

As the name suggests, a traditional customer relationship management system focuses on developing and maintaining relationships by meeting the needs of the customers. It uses advanced technologies to organize, automate, and integrate different business components such as marketing, sales, and customer service. But how is Dynamics 365 CRM different from others?

■ The significant difference between a Dynamics 365 CRM and the others is that it is a cloud-based platform that enables users to access it.

■ All the different kinds of apps are integrated with this system. It supports all Dynamics 365 apps and Microsoft apps, including Office 365, Excel, and Power Board, and enables you to use different apps at the same time without any problems or delays.

Let's move on to the Dynamics 365 CRM applications:

■ **Dynamics 365 Sales.** Dynamics 365 Sales provides data and digital tools to your sales teams to turn relationships into revenue. It empowers the sales team to build relationships; evolves using adaptable, scalable, and easy-to-use sales solutions; and maximizes productivity with intelligent automation.

■ **Dynamics 365 Customer Service.** Dynamics 365 Customer Service ensures that your team gets the right tools and streamlined data in a unified platform to intelligently handle requests and complex issues, to deliver authenticated personalized experience, and to earn customer loyalty for life.

■ **Dynamics 365 Field Service.** Dynamics 365 Field Service is a proactive application that enables your technicians to monitor every piece of customer equipment remotely. If any issue arises with the equipment, the technician proactively takes action to resolve the issue by scheduling the appointment with the customer for on-site service, thus empowering your organization to deliver maximum quality service with a seamless end-to-end experience.

▪ **Dynamics 365 Marketing** Dynamics 365 Marketing is an application that helps you to plan, automate, and monitor all the prospects that can turn into qualified marketing leads. It enables you to automate marketing processes such as email campaigns, prioritize your leads, design interactive online forms, generate and score leads, share information seamlessly across teams, and much more all in one place.

Enterprise Resource Planning

Businesses need an ERP system to manage core business operations and improve data perceptibility around finance data management and manufacturing. How is the Dynamics 365 ERP system different from others? Dynamics 365 has connected both CRM and ERP systems to reduce information silos. By integrating CRM and ERP systems, it saves employees the trouble of having to make data entries on both systems individually. Dynamics 365 provides connectors that enable both systems to communicate with each other.

Let's investigate Dynamics 365 ERP applications:

▪ **Dynamics 365 Commerce.** Dynamics 365 Commerce is an e-commerce solution that enables you to deliver personalized shopping experiences across various physical and digital channels. It helps you build an omnichannel website that can connect all your stores to understand customer needs by monitoring their behavior. It also improves operational efficiency to upscale your business.

- **Dynamics 365 Finance.** Dynamics 365 Finance is a tool that automates and unifies all your global financial operations and predicts future outcomes to make data-driven decisions smarter and faster to drive business growth. It monitors performance in real time to optimize operational expenses with budget control and financial planning and analysis.
- **Dynamics 365 Human Resources.** Dynamics 365 Human Resources is an application that empowers employees to proactively enhance their careers by landing the best candidates using easy-to-use human resources (HR) tools. It helps them in optimizing HR programs, making better decisions using valuable insights, and improving organizational agility for impactful results.
- **Dynamics 365 Supply Chain Management.** Dynamics 365 Supply Chain Management is a tool that enables you to build a unified and resilient supply chain with the ability to provide business intelligence that can help you to innovate manufacturing operations, extend the life of your assets, improve warehouse management, and enhance workforce performance.

Dynamics 365 for Small and Medium-Sized Businesses

Dynamics 365 Business Central is an all-in-one management solution for organizations across a spectrum of business processes used for managing sales, customer service, marketing, finance, and operations. It helps organizations to stay connected with customers in real time and make smarter decisions faster. It is possible to integrate and adapt business processes effortlessly with Dynamics 365 Business Central.

Common Data Model

Businesses use multiple applications for different business processes, such as marketing, sales, and manufacturing that lead to a poorly planned architecture that holds back organizations from scaling in the long term. The employees are wasting time navigating data from one application to another, which increases manual errors and loss of credibility. The only solution to this problem is an integrated system that empowers employees to share data across the spectrum of business applications. Therefore, businesses are switching to Dynamics 365.

But how does Dynamics 365 connect these applications? The answer is the Common Data Model. It is one of the foundations on which Dynamics 365 is built. It provides a shared data language for all the business processes to use. The Common Data Model meta-data system consists of a set of standardized predefined schemas, including entities, attributes, semantic metadata, and relationships, that make it possible to share data across Microsoft Power Apps, Power BI, Dynamics 365, and Azure. Because of this, organizations can achieve semantic and structural consistency across applications.

INTRODUCTION TO POWER PLATFORM

Businesses are harnessing large amounts of data every second from sources such as social media, web, and business systems like Dynamics 365 ERP/CRM. How can this data be used to gain insights and drive intelligent business processes? This is where the Power Platform comes in.

What Is Power Platform?

Power Platform is a collective term for four Microsoft products: (1) Power BI, (2) PowerApps, (3) Power Automate, and (4) Power Virtual Agents.

Now let's understand why it was invented.

Power Platform can be used with Office 365 and Dynamics 365 (as well as other third-party apps and other Microsoft services) to automate and analyze data easily. It enables end-users who are not technically sound to access digital information. These are the people

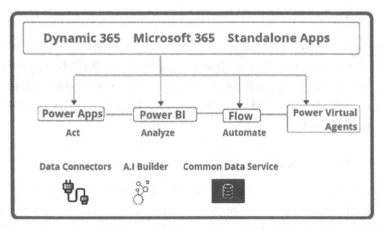

FIGURE 1.1 Understanding the three tools of the Power Platform.

who have a vision and are willing to create something better by using a Triple-A-Loop – analyze, act, and automate – to derive valuable business outcomes. (See Figure 1.1.)

Power Apps

PowerApps is a platform for nontechnical users to develop user-friendly and functional apps without writing a single line of code or low-code application.

It is also known as the Citizen Application Development Platform. The natural connection between Power BI and PowerApps makes it effortless to take actions directly from Power BI reports and dashboards. It increases productivity and makes your work less tedious by avoiding the need to switch between separate apps or copy and paste data from one window to another.

Power Automate

Power Automate is an intelligent process that allows you to automate complex business processes without any technical knowledge of doing so. It has a simple, user-friendly interface through which users can create automated workflows that can be triggered by utilizing insights from Power BI, apps built with PowerApps, or third-party applications.

Power BI

Power BI is a self-service business analytics software solution that pulls data from various business systems with built-in support by the Power Platform such as Dynamics 365, Excel spreadsheets, the cloud, data centers, and other resources. This data is then analyzed for valuable insights.

Power Virtual Agents

A power virtual agent is a low- or no-code graphical interface that empowers you to create chatbots even if you don't have any prior coding experience. It can be used for engaging customers from different business processes such as human resources, sales, or any social platform like Facebook or Skype.

Cross-Cutting Features

The key components of the Power Platform that we just talked about are dependent on the following core services:

- Dataverse
- Connectors
- AI Builder
- Dynamics 365 Customer Voice (previously known as Forms Pro)

These core services enable the components of the Power Platform to do their work.

Dataverse

Organizations use different business applications for different purposes, and a lot of data is collected from users stored in separate silos. But to automate business processes or build new applications, we need to bring the data from all the applications in one place. This is where Dataverse comes in (previously known as Dataverse).

Dataverse environment is like a secure database system that allows you to store and manage data across business applications.

It has a built-in set of standard entities that are used to store data. It also enables you to build custom entities as per your business requirements that can be accessed using a power query.

Connectors

Dataverse does not exactly have all the data within; the concept of connectors was implemented. As the name suggests, connectors connect different applications or services. For example, imagine the data stored in all of your business applications are in different languages. Then, what do you need here? It would be best if you had a common guide that can translate the language for the system you want to connect to, so the connectors do the work.

It enables Power apps to effectively communicate with data from other systems and services without knowing the APIs or the interfaces involved. Microsoft provides over 300 built-in connectors, and you can also build custom connectors as per your business needs.

AI Builder

An AI Builder is the new capability of Power Platform that enables you to intuitively add AI capabilities within your business applications to automate processes and predict outcomes. Like the Power Platform, AI Builder doesn't need coding experience to create custom AI solutions. It helps you to create the AI model, which can be used to keep track of all your products by using object detection. It also helps you to predict future outcomes from the data already available in your business apps so that you can make intelligent decisions to drive the growth of your business.

Dynamics 365 Customer Voice

Successful businesses understand that the customer's feedback is a crucial point for the growth of the business. Every business website has a feedback form where you can ask your queries or write your product experience. But Dynamics 365 Customer Voice is providing something more. It provides your organization with some additional capabilities, such as the ability to create a survey and share it with your customers for valuable feedback. Once the responses are received, Power BI analyzes feedback about your products and services to evaluate the information and take actions to transform products and employee experiences.

Unlike the past, people are now connected through social media and communication solutions. Therefore, businesses are beginning to realize the potential of data-driven decisions, large-scale coordination, and the efficiency of online tools. Thus, Power Platform tools play an important role in improving productivity and automating business processes. To unlock the true potential of Dynamics 365 and Power Platform tools, this book will show you how you can do wonders in your business by using machine learning with these two technologies. It is an important topic because it will help you to make proactive decisions for your business by using predictive data analytics. It also allows businesses to utilize future predictions to perform operations more efficiently. Now let's look at how adding a layer of intelligence to Dynamics 365 and Power platform using machine learning would benefit the businesses.

Whether it's sending follow-up emails, similar record creation, or scheduling and managing appointments, isn't it frustrating to do the same task at your workplace every day?

Just imagine that your employee takes 5 minutes for a repetitive task of sending follow-up emails to all the possible prospects every day. This means he spends 125 minutes, or 2 hours in a month, considering a month has, on average, 25 working days. In a year, that employee will spend 1,500 minutes or 25 hours. If your organization has 100 such employees, imagine how many productive hours your business will lose. Think about how much your business would have achieved if these employees had worked on tasks that demanded their skills. What if you could reduce these numbers by using machine learning in Dynamics 365?

Dynamics 365 has a feature of email engagement in a sales insight suite that sends you an alert when recipients open your email, click a link in your email, open an attachment sent in email, or give a reply. The activities it doesn't do on its own that require manual work are:

- It doesn't send a follow-up email on its own.
- It doesn't automatically set a time to send a follow-up email.

Sure, Dynamics 365 does give you the facility to create an appropriate email template based on your organization's previous email interaction history. But choosing the right follow-up template and setting time for a follow-up email is still manual work. These two problems can be solved by using machine learning in Dynamics 365.

Machine learning has an algorithm called a predictive time algorithm that will help you to set optimal open times for every recipient. For this, a machine should have the recipient's past data, including time engaged with opens and clicks on the links sent in previous emails. This way, a machine will learn what's the best time to send a follow-up email and will set an alert in Dynamics 365.

The second problem can be resolved by a sentiment analysis of email responses by using machine learning (ML) techniques with natural language processing (NLP). ML, if provided with large datasets, can effectively classify the sentiments of email within minutes using precise algorithms. This will help the machine to automatically send appropriate follow-up emails to recipients on the optimal time already set by the machine.

How amazing it would be if all these repetitive tasks are performed by a machine so that you can channel your energy and time on a more complex and productive task.

WHAT IS MACHINE LEARNING: HOW HAS IT EVOLVED?

"The early bird gets the first worm, but the wisest bird gets the fastest one."

— *Matshona Dhliwayo*

Hard work can take you wherever you want, but smart work can make you reach there faster. Let's make our system smart enough to carry out repetitive/mundane tasks. Now, let's understand what machine learning is all about and how it can make a difference.

Machine learning is like a person learning from experience. For example, as the owner of a grocery store, you need to optimize your inventory. The question is, how can ML help you in doing so? ML can predict inventory needs based on the weekday, season, events in nearby locations, customers' behavior, and so on. But for precise predictions, you need to feed your machine with lots of data, so that machine learning algorithms find patterns in the data. Using this data, the ML algorithm can predict sales in advance. Also, if you are using computer vision technology to monitor customer behavior or if you are using a robot assistant like LoweBot in your store, both technologies help ML to keep track of inventory and notify managers if any unexpected pattern of inventory data is found.

 ## DEFINITION OF MACHINE LEARNING

Machine learning unlocks the hidden insight of data by allowing machines to learn from examples and experiences. Instead of writing the code explicitly, what you do is feed the data to the generic algorithms in the machines. The machines then analyze this data, change the data patterns, and build the logic to serve predictions on previously unseen data.

Evolution of Machine Learning

Ever imagine what business was like 50 years ago when there were no computing machines? We can thank those genius philosophers, mathematicians, and computer scientists who made what was once fiction a reality. Today, the technology that helps us do everything from housecleaning to driving cars is no longer science fiction. Machine learning helps all businesses and individuals to improve decision making, detect diseases, increase productivity, navigate vehicles and suggest the fastest route after analyzing traffic patterns, forecast weather, detect fraud, and much more.

Figure 1.2 shows the journey of how technology came together and how machine learning evolved.

The constant evolution of ML from robotic process automation to technical expertise has made its mark in many sectors. All businesses, ranging from start-ups to global multinationals, want to develop a robust ML strategy in an increasingly ambitious and technical market.

Currently, businesses are working to achieve the following: advancement in cybersecurity, regulation of digital data, and faster

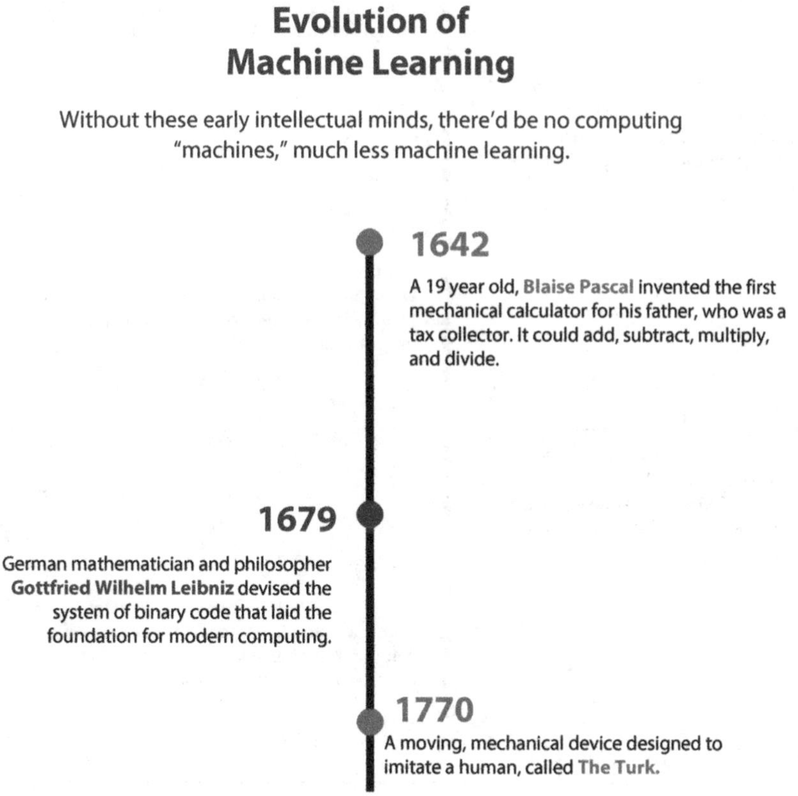

Evolution of Machine Learning

Without these early intellectual minds, there'd be no computing "machines," much less machine learning.

1642

A 19 year old, Blaise Pascal invented the first mechanical calculator for his father, who was a tax collector. It could add, subtract, multiply, and divide.

1679

German mathematician and philosopher Gottfried Wilhelm Leibniz devised the system of binary code that laid the foundation for modern computing.

1770

A moving, mechanical device designed to imitate a human, called The Turk.

FIGURE 1.2   Evolution of machine learning.

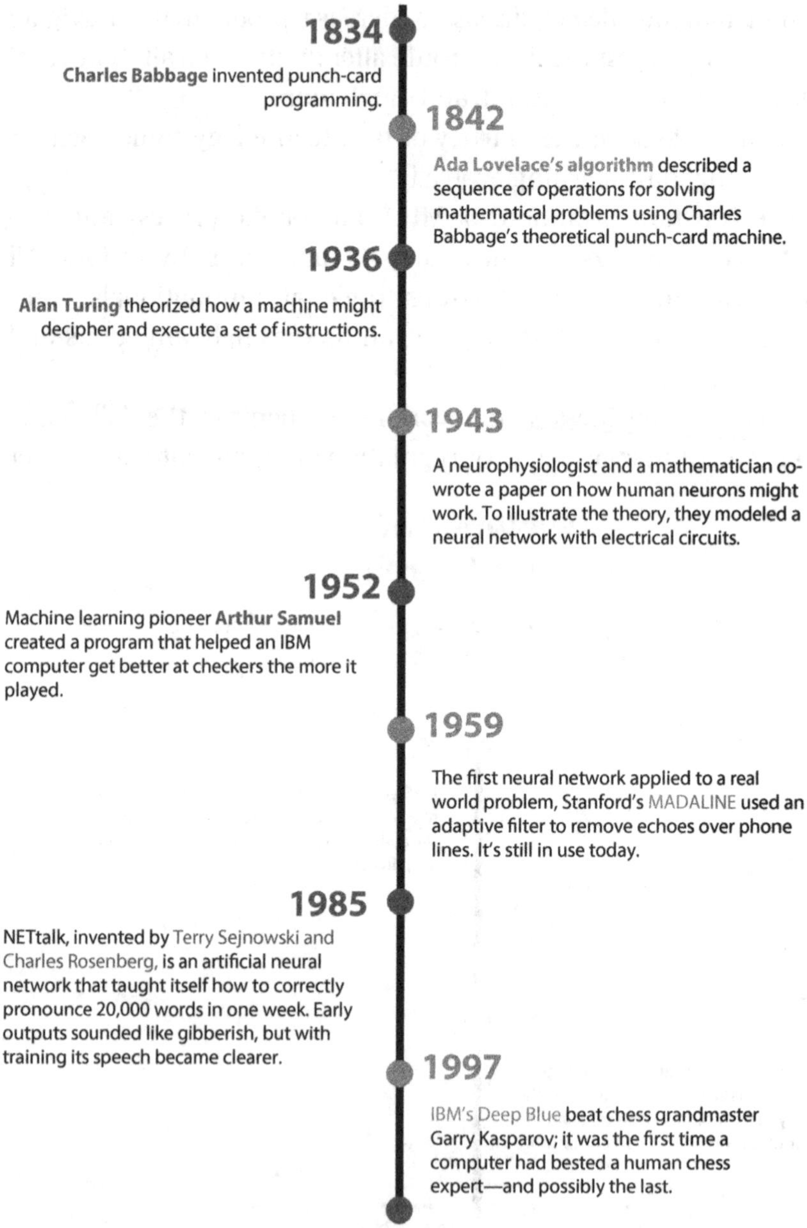

1834
Charles Babbage invented punch-card programming.

1842
Ada Lovelace's algorithm described a sequence of operations for solving mathematical problems using Charles Babbage's theoretical punch-card machine.

1936
Alan Turing theorized how a machine might decipher and execute a set of instructions.

1943
A neurophysiologist and a mathematician co-wrote a paper on how human neurons might work. To illustrate the theory, they modeled a neural network with electrical circuits.

1952
Machine learning pioneer Arthur Samuel created a program that helped an IBM computer get better at checkers the more it played.

1959
The first neural network applied to a real world problem, Stanford's MADALINE used an adaptive filter to remove echoes over phone lines. It's still in use today.

1985
NETtalk, invented by Terry Sejnowski and Charles Rosenberg, is an artificial neural network that taught itself how to correctly pronounce 20,000 words in one week. Early outputs sounded like gibberish, but with training its speech became clearer.

1997
IBM's Deep Blue beat chess grandmaster Garry Kasparov; it was the first time a computer had bested a human chess expert—and possibly the last.

FIGURE 1.2   Continued

From theory, It all became real.

Machine learning moves out of the lab and into our lives
with applications across industries.

2006

Geoffrey Hinton re-branded neural net
research as "deep learning." Today, the
internet's heaviest hitters use his techniques
to improve tools like voice recognition and
image tagging.

2009

ImageNet created by Fei-Fei Li from Stanford
University as large visual database, who realized
that the best machine learning algorithms
wouldn't work well if the data didn't reflect the
real world.

2011

IBM's Watson computer won at *Jeopardy!* by
powering a computerized doctor's assistant.

2012

A neural network created by Google learned to
recognize humans and cats without ever being
told how to characterize either.

2014

Chatbot "Eugene Goostman" passed the
Turing Test. It convinced 33% of human
judges that it was a Ukrainian teen.

2014

Healthtech began using event simulation to
predict ER wait times based on data like
staffing levels, medical histories, and hospital
layouts. These predictions help hospitals
reduce the wait, a key factor in better patient
outcomes.

2015

Google's AlphaGo was the first program to
best a professional player at Go, considered
the most difficult board game in the world.

FIGURE 1.2   Continued

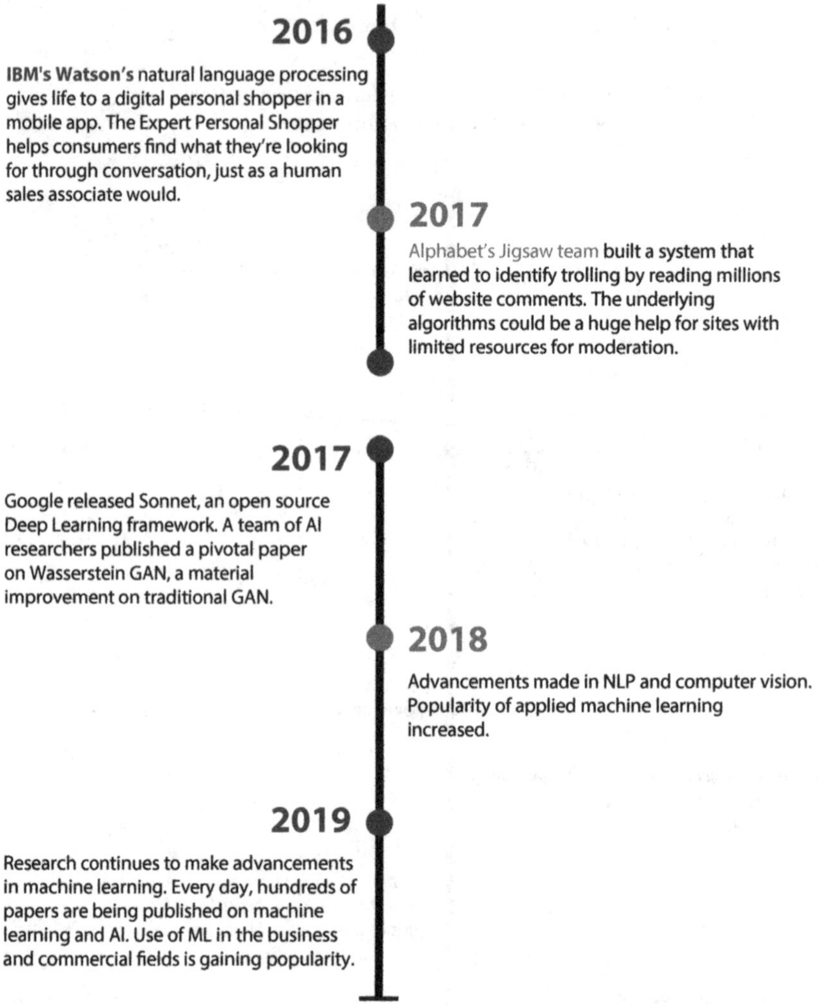

2016

IBM's **Watson's** natural language processing gives life to a digital personal shopper in a mobile app. The Expert Personal Shopper helps consumers find what they're looking for through conversation, just as a human sales associate would.

2017

Alphabet's Jigsaw team **built a system that learned to identify trolling by reading millions of website comments. The underlying algorithms could be a huge help for sites with limited resources for moderation.**

2017

Google released Sonnet, an open source Deep Learning framework. A team of AI researchers published a pivotal paper on Wasserstein GAN, a material improvement on traditional GAN.

2018

Advancements made in NLP and computer vision. Popularity of applied machine learning increased.

2019

Research continues to make advancements in machine learning. Every day, hundreds of papers are being published on machine learning and AI. Use of ML in the business and commercial fields is gaining popularity.

FIGURE 1.2 Continued

computing power. In the following chapters, this book will teach you to utilize advanced ML solutions in Dynamics 365 for executing complex tasks and sustaining accuracy for the success of businesses.

Lifecycle of Machine Learning

Data-driven organizations face different challenges in developing ML models, from prototyping to production. To derive practical business values, data scientists and data engineers serve the model with a huge amount of data and train it to take advantage of ML algorithms. To create a desirable ML system, businesses need to comprehend the ML lifecycle process. Now let's understand why ML lifecycle is so important for businesses.

According to sas.com, 50 percent of models never make it to production due to the following reasons:

- **Insufficient data.** Insufficient data, when fed to the model, result in an increase in variance. Variance is a value that is equal to the difference between the prediction accuracy of training data and test data in the ML model. If the prediction accuracy between training data and test data is high, the model will produce accurate results with training data but will stop working as soon as test data is fed into it.
- **Nonrepresentative training data.** It is the training set of data that doesn't reflect the cases of the deployment environment. This problem is also called sampling bias. It is necessary to make sure that the sample you are feeding to the model matches the environment it's going to be deployed in.
- **Poor quality data.** It refers to the data that has missing observations, errors, outliers (values that deviate from other observations on data), and noise (spurious and unnecessary data).
- **Overfitting the data.** It is a situation when the model learns the detail and noise in the training data so well that it produces negative results when fed with new data.
- **Underfitting the data.** This situation occurs when you want to build an accurate model with fewer data. Due to a lack of data, the model is unable to capture the underlying trend of the data.

So, to build a model, it is crucial to have the right data, at the right time, in the right location. The ML lifecycles play a key role in building custom ML algorithms to support learning models. The main purpose of the lifecycle is to create a model with a good workflow that can be reproduced, revisited, and deployed to production easily.

Now let's understand what the machine learning lifecycle is and how it works:

The machine learning lifecycle is a repetitive process to build an efficient machine learning system called a "model."

The machine learning lifecycle consists of four phases: (1) data preparation, (2) machine learning model, (3) validation, and (4) deployment. This lifecycle is all about gaining deeper insights from data. It is leveraged by data engineers, data scientists, and those working with data to develop, train, validate, and serve machine learning models. Figure 1.3 depicts a typical ML lifecycle and its phases.

Let's jump into these phases one by one.

Data Preparation

Machine learning algorithms need the right data to solve the problem. So first, you need to make sure that the data you have collected is on a useful scale and format. Data preparation is a process that involves converting raw data into a clean dataset before applying machine learning algorithms to the data.

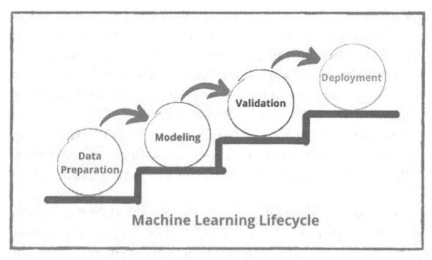

FIGURE 1.3 Machine learning lifecycle.

"The goal is to turn data into information and information into insight."

— *Carly Fiorina*

Data preparation involves four phases (also see Figure 1.4):

1. **Data collection or data selection.** The performance of the model solely depends on how effectively it can achieve accuracy, precision, classification, anomaly detection, and recommendation. This step involves gathering the subset of all available data from multiple resources within your organization. It's not always a good idea to include all the data that is available. The key is to select quality data. People always think that more is better. But while selecting data, you need to strongly address the problem you are working on. For example, you need your model to predict the travel time information of a vehicle for a given expressway by predicting the average speed of the expressway in the future.

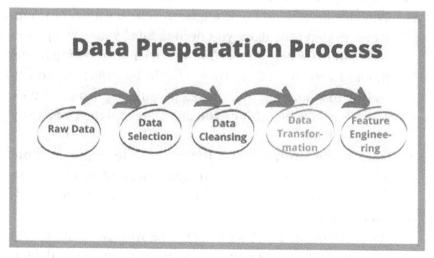

FIGURE 1.4   Data preparation process.

This problem definition does not provide any specific inputs that should be taken into consideration, so it is important to create a list of feasible inputs and output variables. To estimate the average speed of the expressway in the future, you need to map past data in the model. Past data should include the theoretical knowledge of the transportation system, user behavior, user statistics, traffic on business days and on weekends, traffic at daytime and nighttime, and so on.

To select quality data, make some assumptions and be sure of the solution you want from your model. However, the process of collecting data is actually a really important step in the ML lifecycle. And all the different decisions that you have to make while collecting data can end up having a pretty big effect on your model results.

2. **Data cleansing.** To cleanse your data, you first need to understand your data. To gain valuable insights, you need quality data, but the raw data consist of incorrect or missing values. So relevant data must be sourced and cleansed. There are two key stages of selecting relevant data from raw data:

a. **Data assessment.** It is a task to evaluate the feasibility of available data and how it aligns to your business problem. To understand the data, you need to label your examples in an appropriate category so that the machine learning model should learn to predict. There should be sufficient data to build a machine learning model because the usage of data depends on the algorithms you are using and the complexity of the problem.

b. **Data exploration.** This is the phase to test your assumption and to create meaningful summaries of your data. In this phase, you search for missing values, outliers, and unbalanced data.

Data cleansing is a process that deals with issues occurring in raw data such as missing values, outliers, unbalanced data, typos in data, duplicate data, and so on. Let's see how data is cleaned in this stage:

a. **Missing values.** If your data has missing values, then you should explore the reason behind it to decide whether or not it is possible to drop these data points as a whole. If dropping data points is not an option, then impute the substitute values in place of missing data.

b. **Outliers.** Outliers are the values that differ from other observations in the data. To deal with outliers, you need to impute alternate values to make it useful for your machine learning model. You can use algorithms such as random forest or gradient boosted trees.

c. **Unbalanced data.** Unbalanced data refers to the lack of a similar number of examples. For instance, to detect fraud, you need to have the same number of fraud cases as normal cases, as we know that machine learning learns from examples. So, if your data lack in fraud cases, it will be difficult for a ML model to identify it. So, it is necessary to have balanced data.

3. **Data transformation.** Data transformation plays an important role in making data constructive so that it can be used in the model. It is performed to increase the probability of algorithms making precise and meaningful predictions. There are several data transformation techniques such as:

   ▪ **Categorical encoding.** Machine learning models are mathematical models that understand numeric representation, but categorical data has label values. Some of the ML algorithms require input and output variables to be numeric. So, for this reason, categorical data is converted to numerical data using either of these two steps:

      i. **Integer encoding.** Also known as label coding, it assigns an integer value to every unique category. Machine learning algorithms are capable of understanding this relationship between integer and category. For example, your qualification can be high school, college, or postgraduate. If we assign an integer to each of these categories like high school = 1, college = 2, postgraduate = 3, this data will become machine-readable.

ii. **One-hot encoding**. One-hot encoding is used when the categorical variables don't have an ordinal relationship. In one-hot encoding, the binary value is assigned to each unique value and is separated by different columns. For example, Facebook has a relationship status feature—engaged, married, separated, divorced, or widowed. Then each status will have different columns with "engaged" status assigned value one in the "engaged" column and zero in the remaining four columns.

■ **Dealing with skewed data.** If your data is not symmetric, meaning if one half of your data distribution is not the mirror image of the other half, then the data is considered as asymmetric or skewed data. So, to discover patterns in skewed data, you need to apply a log transformation or reciprocals (i.e., positive or negative) or Box-Cox transformation over the whole set of values. This way, you can use it for the statistical model.

■ **Bias mitigation.** Bias mitigation can be done by alternating current values and labels to get a more unbiased model. Some algorithms that can help in this process are reweighing, optimized preprocessing, learning fair representations, and disparate impact remover.

■ **Scaling.** When you use regression algorithms and algorithms using Euclidean distances, you need to transform your data into a particular range. This can be done by altering the values of each numerical feature and setting it to a common scale. This can be done by using normalization (min-max scaling) or z-score standardization.

4. **Feature engineering.** Feature engineering is a process of constructing explanatory variables and features from raw data to

turn our inputs into a machine-readable format. These variables and features are used to train the model. To follow this step, one should have a clear understanding of the data. Feature engineering can be achieved in two activities:

a. **Feature extraction**. It is done to reduce the number of processing resources without losing relevant information. This activity combines variables to features, thus reducing the amount of processing data while still accurately describing the original dataset.

b. **Capturing feature relationships.** If you have a better understanding of your data, you can find out the relationship between two features so as to help your algorithm focus on what you know is important.

Select Algorithm and Model (Modeling)

After the completion of the tough part, that is, data selection and data pre-processing, we are now moving to the interesting part: modeling.

Modeling is an iterative process of creating a smart model by continuously training and testing the model until you discover the one with high accuracy and performance.

To train an ML model, you need to provide an ML algorithm with a clean training dataset to learn from. Choosing a learning algorithm depends on the problem at hand. The training data that you are planning to feed to the ML algorithm must contain the target attribute. ML algorithms find patterns in training data and learn from it. This ML model is then tested with new data to make predictions for the unknown target attribute. Let's understand it with an example.

You want to train your model to separate spam mails from your regular emails. To do so, you need to provide your learning algorithm with the training data that contains a white list and black list. The white list contains email addresses of people you tend to receive email from. The blacklist contains all the addresses of users that you want to avoid receiving email from. So, the ML algorithm will learn from this training data and predict if the new mail is from black list or white list. If it's from the black list, it automatically labels it as spam.

To create an effective model, it is important to select an accurate algorithm that can find predictable, repeatable patterns. On the one hand, some problems that need ML are very specific and require a unique approach to solve the problem, On the other hand, some problems need a trial-and-error approach.

Machine learning algorithms are divided into four main types (see Figure 1.5):

1. Supervised learning
2. Unsupervised learning
3. Semi-supervised learning
4. Reinforcement learning

Let's learn them one by one:

1. **Supervised learning.** It's a learning algorithm in which the machine is trained with data that is well labeled and predicts with the help of a labeled dataset.

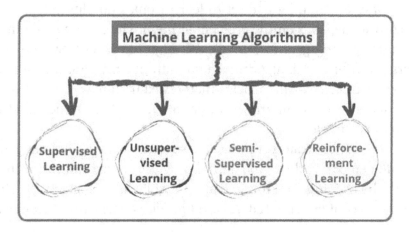

FIGURE 1.5 Machine learning algorithms.

What is labeled data? The data for which you already know the target answer is called labeled data. For example, if I show you an image and tell you that it is a butterfly, then it's called labeled data. However, if I show you an image without telling you what it is, that is referred to as unlabeled data.

Now let's understand with an example how labeled data makes a machine learn.

We have images that are labeled as spoon and knife; we then feed them to the machine, which analyzes and learns the association of these images with their labels based on their features such as shape, size, and sharpness. Now, if any new image is fed to the machine without any label, the past data helps the machine to predict accurately and tell whether it's a spoon or knife. Thus, in supervised machine learning, the algorithm teaches the model to learn from the labeled example that we provide.

It consists of two techniques: classification and regression.

a. **Classification.** For example, if the output variable is categorical such as red or blue, disease or no disease, male or female, will I get an increment or not?

b. **Regression.** Regression is a problem when the output variable is a real or a continuous value, for example, salary based on work experience or weight based on height. So, it creates predictive models showing trends in data. For example, how much increment will I get?

The following is a list of commonly used algorithms in supervised learning:

- Nearest neighbor
- Naive Bayes
- Decision trees
- Linear regression
- Support vector machines (SVM)
- Neural networks
- Logistic regression
- Linear discriminant analysis
- Similarity learning

2. **Unsupervised learning**. In this learning, no training is given to the machine, allowing it to act on data that is not labeled. Hence, the machine tries to identify the patterns and provide the predictions. Let's take the example of a spoon and knife, but this time we do not tell the machine whether it's a spoon or a knife. The machine by itself identifies patterns from the set and makes a group based on their patterns, similarities, differences, and so on.

   Unsupervised learning consists of two techniques: clustering and association.

   a. **Clustering.** In clustering, the machine forms groups based on the behavior of the data. For example, which customer made similar product purchases?

   b. **Association.** It is an area of machine learning that identifies exceptional relationships between variables in large datasets. For example, which products were purchased together?

   The following is a list of commonly used algorithms in unsupervised learning:
   - k-means clustering
   - Association rules

3. **Semi-supervised learning**. Semi-supervised learning is a type of machine learning that uses a combination of both supervised and unsupervised learning techniques. It is used in a scenario where our dataset is a combination of both labeled and unlabeled data.

   For example, let's assume that we have access to a large number of unlabeled datasets that we like to train a model on. Manually labeling the whole data by ourselves is just not practical. So, instead of labeling the whole dataset, we manually label some parts of the dataset ourselves and use that portion to train our model. But this way, all the unlabeled data will be of no use. As we know, the more data we have to train our model, the better and more robust our model would be. So what can we do to use the unlabeled data of our dataset?

This is why semi-supervised learning was introduced. To prevent our unlabeled data from getting wasted, we can implement a technique of semi-supervised learning called pseudo labeling.

To understand pseudo labeling, let's continue with the example mentioned previously.

Our model is trained using labeled data, and it is performing pretty well. Everything to this point is just regular supervised learning. Now we will use unsupervised learning to predict the remaining unlabeled portion of data. We will serve the unlabeled data to our model. The trained model will then process this data, and as a result, it will predict individual outputs for each piece of unlabeled data. Thus, pseudo labeling is a process of labeling the unlabeled data with the output that is predicted by our neural network. With pseudo labeling, we can train on an audaciously larger dataset.

4. **Reinforcement learning**. There is no predefined data in reinforcement learning. It is the area of machine learning that is concerned with behavioral psychology. In this learning, an agent is put into an environment, and he learns to behave in this environment by performing certain actions and observing the awards that they get from their actions. Reinforcement learning involves software agents that take appropriate actions in a particular situation to earn maximum rewards. There is no expected output in this learning. The reinforcement agent decides what actions to take to perform a task. In the absence of the training dataset, it is bound to learn from its own experience.

The following is a list of commonly used algorithms in reinforcement learning:

■ Q-learning
■ Temporal difference (TD)
■ Deep adversarial networks

Now to choose which algorithm is right for your problem, you should categorize your problem according to the following:

- Categorize by input
  - Labeled data: supervised learning
  - Unlabeled data: unsupervised learning
  - Combination of labeled and unlabeled data: semi-supervised learning
  - No data and want to optimize an objective function by interacting with an environment: reinforcement learning
- Categorize by output
- If the output of a model is a number: regression problem
- If the output of a model is a class: classification problem
- If the output of your model is a set of input groups: clustering problem
- To detect an anomaly: anomaly detection
- Understand your constraints
  - Storage capacity of model
  - Fast prediction
  - Fast learning
- **Find the available algorithms:** Factors affecting the choice of the model are:
  - Business goals
  - Amount of preprocessing required in data
  - Accuracy of the model
  - Scalability of the model
- Consider model complexity
  - Complex feature engineering
  - Computational overhead

These points can help you to choose the right algorithm for developing a solution to a real-time business problem that requires knowledge of business requirements, rules and regulations, and stakeholders' interests as well as significant expertise. Hence, to solve a machine problem, it is crucial to combine and balance algorithms for valuable results.

Validation

Once the machine learning model has been properly trained on a given dataset, then we have to test the model. In this step, we check for the accuracy of the model by rendering a test dataset to it. Testing the model is important to find out the percentage accuracy of the model as per the project requirement or given problem.

The input of this validation stage is the trained model produced by the earlier step in the model learning stage, and the output is a validated model that provides enough information to allow users to check whether the machine learning model is appropriate for its intended purpose. Thus, this validation stage of the machine learning lifecycle deals with whether the model is working properly as desired or not when fed with unseen inputs. Thus, model validation is the process that evaluates a trained model on a test dataset. This step renders the generalization ability of the trained model.

Deployment

The last step of the machine learning lifecycle is deployment, where we deploy the ML model in the real-world system. Deployment is a very crucial step in the machine learning lifecycle process. Deployment is a process of making your model available to make predictions in the production environment. The aim of this stage is to check the proper functionality of the model post-deployment. The models need to be deployed in such a way that they can be used for inference as well as be updated regularly. If the prepared model produces an accurate result as per the specified requirements, with acceptable speed, only then do we deploy the model in the real system. But before deploying the project, you need to check whether it is improving its performance using available data or not and whether you want to go with a Platform as a Service (PaaS) or Infrastructure as a Service (IaaS). A PaaS is excellent for prototyping and businesses with lower traffic. Eventually, when the business grows and traffic increases, you need to switch to IaaS. This is the step to test the ability to predict outcomes in the real world.

Advantages of Machine Learning

Machine learning can help you solve your business issues by predicting future outcomes and make better decisions accordingly. Here are some advantages that can help you understand if machine learning is for you:

- Extract meaningful insights from a large volume of data. For example, ML helps in discovering specific patterns from a large volume of data that would not be plausible to humans (e.g., an e-commerce website like Flipkart has a large volume of data. Using ML, it observes the purchasing and browsing history of the customer, discovers a pattern from it, and then recommends similar products and deals to them).
- Algorithms self-improve the prediction without any manual support.
- Machine learning algorithms can learn from experience. So, the accuracy of predictions also improves as the project grows.
- Machine learning algorithms can handle a variety of data. For example, multidimensional data.
- Machine learning automates time-intensive and repetitive tasks.
- Machine learning helps businesses to make the right decisions by constantly monitoring the change in market demands and facilitating organizations to take proactive measures to maintain their competing edge in real time.

Drawbacks of Machine Learning

Now that we are aware of all the advantages of machine learning, Let's uncover some disadvantages, as every coin has two sides:

- Requires massive datasets to train machine learning algorithms.
- Running training data on each algorithm to select the right algorithm for your problem is a time-consuming and manual task.
- Training and testing the huge datasets in all of the algorithms can cause errors that take a lot of time to resolve.

Machine Learning + Dynamics 365 / Power Platform: Insights Everywhere

A key point that we would like to cover in this book is really to give you insights about what is important for the decade to come: how to go ahead after an implementation of your "basic" CRM and ERP system and enhance it with Dynamics 365 and Power Platform. As you will see in the next chapters, we will bring those two worlds together.

AI is everywhere now, and with the big data you'll have in those systems, it's a shame to not put intelligence behind them. Microsoft is pushing with Insight Add-On, basically to add intelligence directly in the system with the data on it without coding everything.

AI Builder is part of the Power Platform, leveraging directly some AI model just in a few clicks for you. Dynamics 365 Finance Operations with all the modules from every process of the company will be a huge part of AI by addressing these kinds of questions: What is my cash flow forecast, if this customer will pay me on time or not? What is my demand forecast in term of supply chain? Production order? What is my churn score for those customers? This is where we need to go with a real return on investment for the top management of a company. Even Power BI and Azure Synapse Analytics and every kind of new feature in the Microsoft Cloud ecosystem are going now with some AI part and features. So, it's time to jump!

CHAPTER TWO

Artificial Intelligence and Pre-Built Machine Learning in Dynamics 365

 AZURE AI PLATFORM

With the innovations of machine intelligence becoming capable of delivering – and sometimes exceeding – human-level performance in perceptual and cognitive tasks, organizations are increasingly evaluating how artificial intelligence can be applied to derive new business value and change the world for the better. It is fair to assume that soon the companies that are using the technologies to automate all the regular and routine work will progress faster than those that aren't.

Technologies like artificial intelligence (AI) are transforming the way businesses are operating these days. It is the most trending technology of today and along with Azure cloud-based services, it's doing miracles for small- and large-scale organizations.

How is Azure AI helping Dynamics 365 users?

"It's the choices you make that determines your future."

— *Donny Ingram*

Today, AI capabilities can be applied across the business spectrum to build AI-powered business logic and user interfaces. AI capabilities in Dynamics 365 enables businesses to deliver intelligent business decisions, engage customers, optimize operations, empower employees, and transform products.

Azure AI combines the ability to develop AI solutions for all skill levels, build AI into mission-critical applications securely at scale, and put responsible AI into action to understand, protect, and control your AI systems.

Azure AI is both a collection of cloud-based AI models called Azure Cognitive Services and a Python-based machine learning service called Azure Machine Learning. Azure Cognitive Services are domain-specific, pre-trained AI models that can be customized with your data and deployed in the cloud and the edge. Azure Machine Learning empowers developers and data scientists of all skill levels to build, train, and deploy machine learning models, optimize and accelerate model inferencing, speed up model development with Automated Machine Learning, and easily deploy and manage your models across the cloud and the edge.

Azure AI empowers the developers and data scientists of millions of organizations around the world to build innovative solutions. Using Azure AI, businesses can easily embed powerful tools like Cognitive Services, Bot Framework, Azure Machine Learning, and many more to their applications.

Azure AI intends to provide AI capabilities in three key areas:

1. To quickly build and easily train, deploy, and manage your models with Azure Machine Learning to optimize business processes.
2. To deliver breakthrough experiences in your AI-powered apps and agents with vision, speech, language understanding, and decision-making capabilities.
3. To build knowledge mining solutions to unlock insights from all unstructured content using Azure Cognitive Search.

Let's start with machine learning (ML).

Machine Learning

Why do we need machine learning for our businesses?

Let's imagine that you own an online e-commerce business, and a lot of decisions are made in every business to run it successfully. Surely you also have a decision-making tool that could be a part of dynamics or it could be a separate tool. And as it is an e-commerce website, all your product catalogs reside in it. Now, what are the decisions that need to be made by decision management tools?

- When a customer logs in to your website with his account, what products should be shown to him? Either you can show all the products residing on your website or you can personalize the experience by showing only those products which might interest him.

    Consider that the decision-making tool showed only those products that might grab his interest. Now the customer made a choice and added the product into a cart.
- Here comes our second decision that needs to be made: Based on his selection of the first product, what other products can you recommend that he could buy together?
- Or, what similar products of other brands can you show that match the customer's expectations?

As we can see, a simple business process also involves a lot of decision making. Developers used to code all these decisions, but coding every decision came with its limitations. For instance, if there is any change in the business process, the developer had to go through the code and modify the rules, which seemed to be a lot of work.

Now Dynamics 365 provides some capabilities, for example, in this situation. It uses cross-sell and up-sell techniques and a rule-based engine for making such decisions.

Cross-selling or up-selling is a technique that involves either selling an additional product to the customer or recommending a better one. If Dynamics 365 can take care of these situations, then why machine learning?

If we use ML, it can help us bring intelligence to all such decisions by augmenting these rules, which can result in better predictive or prescriptive analysis that makes your application much more flexible. In this case, by observing the customer's previous purchases and browsing history, machine learning can analyze customer behavior and predict:

- Which personalized products to show when a customer logs in.
- Which products to recommend that can be purchased together.
- What other brands can best match their expectations.

Sure, Dynamics 365 and Power Platform automates your processes but machine learning when combined with Dynamics 365 can provide AI-powered business logic to automate business process or augment human intelligence to make smarter decisions. Through this example you can understand what machine learning can do for your business.

Let's move into why you should choose Azure Machine Learning.

Azure Machine Learning

Azure Machine Learning is a cloud-based environment that:

- Provides a managed cloud-based workstation optimized for your machine learning development environment called Azure Compute Instances. For more demanding or production grade model training, you can use an Azure Machine Learning compute cluster for additional capabilities.
- Allows you to designate a compute target, which is a designated compute resource or environment where you run your training script or host your service deployment. You can deploy these compute targets as a web service to call for real-time inference, periodically as a batch service, or deployed to an IoT device via a Docker container by using Azure IoT Edge.
- Provides flexibility to build and train models in authoring experiences such as Automated ML, or a visual drag-and-drop Designer, or code-first Notebooks with built-in support for open-source tools and frameworks, IDEs like Jupyter and command-line interfaces, or languages such as Python or R.
- Is a pay-per-use facility, which means you only have to pay for the services you use.

Now, let's get into how Azure ML can optimize business processes:

1. **Consume less time in building applications.** Azure ML accelerates the end-to-end machine learning cycle to empower data scientists to deploy models faster by taking advantage of automated tools.
2. **Support multiple frameworks.** Azure ML allows users to choose from a variety of frameworks to create AI models –such as scikit-learn, PyTorch, MXNet, TensorFlow, Chainer, and Keras.

3. **Offers skill independent experience.** Users can build models using a no-code designer, the Python SDK, Jupyter notebooks, VS Code, or their favorite IDE based on the skill level they possess or the authoring experience they prefer.

4. **Using MLOps for communication between data scientists and the operations team.** It is used to automate plenty of processes and produce more valuable insights by eliminating waste.

5. **Compatibility with container orchestration services.** ML service is compatible with Docker, Azure Kubernetes Service, and Azure Container Instances, so it's easy to deploy models to platforms that support the most mission-critical workloads.

As of now, we have determined why Azure Machine Learning solutions are important for business growth. Now, let's focus on what it has to offer.

Machine Learning Studio

It is a graphical web interface that can give you the best of both worlds as it helps you to create custom machine learning applications, even if you know nothing about writing complex code. The people who benefit the most from this service are those who are new to the field.

Let's understand the working of Azure Machine Learning Studio with an example. It's natural to keep track of your monthly expenses and plan accordingly, but how can you be sure that the upcoming month would also have the same fixed expenses? Surely, by fixed expenses, I am pointing out:

■ Home expenses
■ Food expenses
■ Personal expenses
■ Debt obligations

- Health care expenses
- Transportation expenses

These are the basic expenses that every citizen must pay every month. How can you make such predictions that transportation expense, home expense, or any other expense would not rise or fall in the upcoming month? How relieving would it be if you could predict your next month's expenditure and savings in advance? Perhaps, you can find your answer using the Azure Machine Learning Studio. You shouldn't necessarily know about the technology; Azure Machine Learning Studio simplifies the development and deployment of machine learning models and services. Let's do the same with an assumption.

- **Problem definition**: Your house electricity bill comes under your home expenses and is already covered in your budget. It is usually a fixed expense. Now let's consider the factors that can affect its consistent price. From political judgments to weather situations, from natural disasters to unpredictable factors, any of these circumstances can affect your budget for the upcoming month.

  Let's explore the capabilities by authoring a machine learning project within Azure Machine Learning Studio. You can use the studio to manage your assets within your workspace:
  - Models
  - Datasets
  - Datastores
  - Compute resources
  - Notebooks
  - Experiments
  - Run logs
  - Pipelines
  - Pipeline endpoints

■ **Data collection.** Gathering relevant data is the first and the most important step. There are many sample datasets in the Azure Machine Learning Studio. In Azure Machine Learning, you can connect to existing cloud-based storage (like Azure Data Lake Storage or Synapse Analytics) or leverage a dataset from local files (among other options). To reuse and share datasets across experiments in your workspace, you must first register your dataset:

  ■ Sign into Azure Machine Learning studio. If you don't have an Azure subscription, it's now possible to open a free trial account (https://azure.microsoft.com/en-us/free) and create an Azure ML workspace.

  ■ Select Datasets on the left pane under Assets.

  ■ Select + Create dataset then from local files.

  ■ Complete the form to create and register a new dataset.

■ **Data processing.** This is a very important step of the ML life-cycle as it helps to adjust the data according to your needs. There might be some missing values in your data that needs cleaning so that data can be analyzed precisely. For doing so, you need to drag the Clean Missing Data module from the left panel into your experiment and connect it to your data set. Then you need to select Remove entire row option from the cleaning mode drop-down box to either remove the missing (null) values entirely or replace it with some other value. Now run the experiment.

■ **Defining features.** In this step, you will select the columns from your dataset that will be used to predict the price. For this, you will have to choose the Filter Based Feature Selection module, which consists of various algorithms and correlation methods like Pearson's or Kendall's correlation, mutual information scores, chi-squared values, Spearman correlation, and so on, which can be used for the feature selection process. The feature selection process involves applying statistical tests to inputs, given a specified output to determine which columns in your dataset have the greatest predictive power. As a result, the features that you want to pass to the learning algorithm are selected in this process. Using this module will improve the accuracy and effectiveness of classification by helping you to choose the right features.

▪ **Choosing the right algorithm.** Until this step, we have successfully cleaned and processed our data. In this step, we will first split our cleaned dataset into two parts using the Split module. We will train our model using the first half and score the trained model using the rest of it. Now we need to choose the right algorithm to construct a predictive model that can then be trained and tested. Because we have a labeled dataset, we will have two options to choose from: classification and regression. They are the two types of supervised machine learning, which are produced in the Train Model module and can be used as an input to score it. The Score Model module generates the predicted numeric value of our next month's electricity bill. Now drag the Evaluate Model module to your experiment and connect the output of the Score Model module to it. We are using an evaluation model module to measure the accuracy of our trained model. Click on Run to generate the result from the Evaluate Model module.

Creating a predictive model is an iterative process. To get satisfactory results you need to track all the iterations of your experiment. This way you can compare the results of two runs and decide which run produces the most accurate result.

 ## AZURE MACHINE LEARNING SERVICE

The Azure ML service is an open platform to create ML solutions using Python. It provides tools to scale and automate training, deployment, and monitoring of ML models easily and seamlessly.

Before Azure ML Service, machine learning in a production environment required you to bring together a bunch of data services to support the full machine learning lifecycle, for example:

- **Azure blob storage or Azure data lake storage:** These are storage solutions for data. It's important to bring these solutions together because models cannot be trained without data. Azure Data Lake as well as Azure Synapse Analytics were often commonly used to store data/datasets before machine learning.
- **Virtual machines, Azure HDInsight, and Azure Databricks:** These are brought together to run the code.
- **Virtual network:** A virtual network functions as a security boundary, securing your data by isolating your Azure resources from the public internet. You can bring your virtual network to figure out your computing and data in the same virtual network or you can also use Azure virtual network to your on-premises network to securely train your models and access your deployed models for reasoning.
- **Azure key vault:** It is a cloud-hosted service to manage and secure your credentials, authorize access for certificates, and many other secrets. You have full control of the keys to access and encrypt your data. Administrators have the power to grant or revoke access to the keys.
- **Docker containers:** A Docker container image is a stand-alone, executable package of software used to run your experiment repeatedly because it has everything needed to run an application such as a consistent set of ML libraries, code, system tools, and settings. It uses the Azure Container registry, which is a private Docker registry service to store those Docker containers, and puts them inside your virtual network.
- **Azure Kubernetes service:** Is an orchestration service used to deploy, scale, and manage Docker containers and container-based applications across a cluster of container hosts, including them as well in a virtual network.

Bringing all this together in the same virtual network to get machine learning models to work together consumes a lot of time. But Microsoft eliminated this complexity with Azure Machine Learning Service.

> Azure ML Services is a managed infrastructure for experienced data scientists and AI developers who are proficient in Python. It is a service used to build and deploy models, using any tool or framework.

The following are the benefits of using Azure Machine Learning service:

- It provides end-to-end ML lifecycle management.
- It keeps track of all of your experiments.
- It has built-in capabilities like version control and model reproducibility to replicate any experiment by storing everything related to your experiment such as code, config, environment details, parameter settings, and so on.
- It facilitates you to encapsulate your model in a container so that you can deploy it to Azure on-premises or IoT devices. The container in which you encapsulate your model can be easily managed and scaled.
- It has Notebook VM, which is a cloud-based workstation integrated into Azure Machine Learning Service and specifically created for data scientists to make it easy for them to start locally and then easily compute it in Azure. It helps developers and data scientists to perform operations supported by Azure Machine Learning Python SDK using Jupyter notebook.

- It uses popular frameworks like TensorFlow and scikit-learn and offers a powerful toolset to operate ML experiments. It enables you to deploy models into production in a third-party service like Docker.

AI-powered Apps and Agents

From giving a computer vision to your business for inventory tracking to giving personalized e-commerce experiences a human touch or from enabling companies to spot real-time anomalies to extracting critical data from patients' records, you can build intelligent solutions with little or no technical expertise by using Azure Cognitive Services to meet your end-to-end business needs.

Azure combines several services specifically designed to enable developers to easily make use of AI capabilities in building their AI-powered apps and agents. For example:

- Azure Cognitive Services
- Azure Bot services

Azure Cognitive Services

Azure Cognitive Services includes pre-built AI capabilities and cognitive APIs that can be included in your applications to drive business impact without requiring machine-learning expertise. The AI capabilities, such as speech, vision language, and web-search, can help you build intelligent apps. All it takes is a few lines of codes and an API call to embed these abilities into your apps. Azure Cognitive Services include the following capabilities (also see Figure 2.1):

- **Vision:** Allows your apps to understand images and videos.
- **Speech:** Tools to improve speech recognition and identify the speaker.

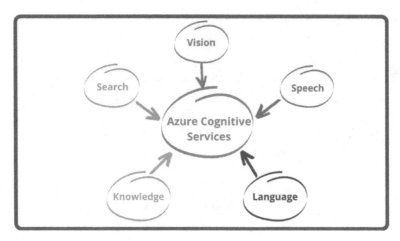

FIGURE 2.1 Azure Cognitive Services.

- **Language:** Understanding sentences and intent rather than just words.
- **Knowledge:** Tracks down research from scientific journals for you.
- **Search:** Applies machine learning to web searches.

Let's get into each of these capabilities.

Vision Vision helps in analyzing videos and images to gain valuable insights. Vision APIs are divided into five parts (computer vision, content moderator, video indexer, face API, and emotion API) (also see Figure 2.2):

1. **Computer vision API** uses image-processing algorithms to process the images intelligently. It can do the following:
   - It can analyze an image by understanding the content within the image. For example, if it's a drawing or a picture, colors in the image.
   - It uses optical character recognition technology to understand the text in the image.

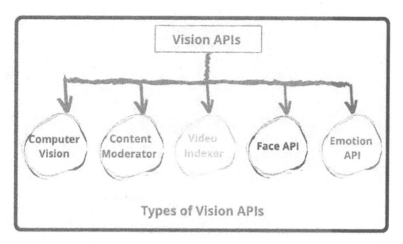

FIGURE 2.2　Types of vision APIs.

- It can retain the key content by scaling and cropping the images.
- With the help of domain-specific models, it can recognize 200,000 celebrities from business, sports, and entertainment all around the world.

Let's look at one of the examples where it is used.

No one likes to handle a paper trail of expenses and receipts. It's good to digitize processes like expense reporting and reimbursement approval to make use of technology for easily handling the most common documents at your workplace that are receipts. When you do expenses in Dynamics 365, you need to take a picture of the receipt and manually fill out all the information such as the time and date of the transaction, merchant information, the amounts of taxes, totals, and so on and then managers spend time in approving these expense reports. Aside from the trouble of auditing these expense reports, it also affects the productivity of your employees. Also, with the escalation of mobile cameras, employees often upload receipt images that are crumpled up, faded, or were taken in a low-quality lighting condition.

To solve these problems, there was a need for a solution to automatically extract all the information there is from receipts that can reduce the manual effort of doing so. Based on vision API, Microsoft introduced a pre-built feature known as Form Recognizer that extracts all the necessary information from the image of the receipts and, thus, reduces the turnaround time to the minimum.

2. **Content moderator API** uses machine learning–assisted classifiers to detect potentially offensive or unwanted images. By this API, you make sure your users are seeing what you want them to. It can perform the following tasks:
   - **Image moderation.** It uses machine learning–based classifiers, custom lists, and OCR to detect offensive images.
   - **Text moderation.** It provides you the capability to detect the obscene language in more than 100 languages and automatically match text against your custom list. It is also helpful in identifying personally identifiable information (PII).
   - **Video moderation.** It uses machine-assisted detection to score possible adult and racy content in videos. It is deployed as a part of Azure media services.

3. **Video indexer.** Video indexer is a video metadata extraction service that helps to put all your intelligence into your videos to unlock valuable insights. With a video indexer, you can get into finding insights immediately after uploading the video and without writing a single line of code. It helps in enhancing content discovery; for example, you can search results by detecting spoken words, faces, emotions, and characters.

4. **Face API.** Face API uses advanced algorithms for the following tasks:
   - **Face detection.** It helps you to detect where the face of a person is in the image. It draws a box around your image detecting your face.
   - **Face verification.** This feature allows you to determine if the two images you are comparing are of the same person or not.

If it doesn't belong to the same person, it tells you the gender and the age of the person.

- ■ **Similar face searching.** This feature allows you to search the face of the same person in a set of images.
- ■ **Face grouping.** It allows you to identify the faces that have similar features and organize them into groups such as by group size.
- ■ **Face identification.** It helps you to detect the other faces in the image and identify who they are. They might be someone you already know.

5. **Emotion API.** Emotional API helps you in recognizing emotions expressed in the images. It detects seven types of emotions (happiness, sadness, surprise, anger, fear, contempt, and neutral expressions) on a face.

Speech

"To understand a language is to understand thoughts."

— *Manali Tiwari*

If you want a machine to understand your thoughts and think like a human, you need to create a solution that understands your speech, your language. Cognitive speech services enable you to do just the same by making your applications useful to an increasingly diverse community around the world. Azure AI capabilities empower your people to improve customer interactions. For example, If you travel across the world to experience different cultures, it's a possibility that you might encounter a situation where you find difficulty communicating with the government officials of that country because your native language is different than theirs. Let's say you visit France, where French is spoken as a native language, and now you want to report a crime. You got mugged and the mugger took your wallet and all the cash in it. How would you explain the situation to a government official?

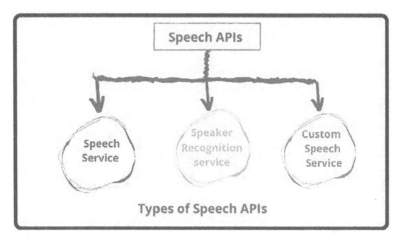

FIGURE 2.3 Types of speech APIs.

If a government official is using Azure speech services to translate speech into text, you have nothing to worry about. Azure speech into text service immediately transcribes audio speech into readable text. This service can be used to investigate the situation; you can tell exactly what happened and at the same time, the government official can ask questions related to the incident.

Cognitive service speech APIs are divided into three categories (also see Figure 2.3):

1. Speech service
2. Speaker recognition service
3. Custom speech service

Let's understand each one of them one by one:

■ **Bing Speech and Speech service.** The Bing Speech API is a unification of algorithms that can process different languages. This API empowers developers to include speech-driven activities in their applications. This API can transcribe real-time interaction with the user.

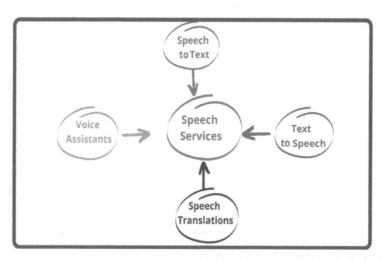

FIGURE 2.4 Speech services.

On January 14, 2020, Microsoft discontinued this API and introduced a much better version known as Speech service. What are the latest features of speech service that Bing Speech didn't have?

- Speech service is an amalgam of all the Azure speech services that previously existed separately such as Custom speech, Speech translation, and Bing Speech.
- Bing Speech didn't have a common speech API and SDK supporting all programming languages and that could run on all modern platforms. This feature is available in speech service.
- Speech service supports C++ SDK, which Bing Speech did not.
- Speech devices SDK consists of a pre-tuned library paired with specific microphone-enabled hardware.

Since Bing Speech has been replaced with Speech service, we will only discuss speech services and its features (see Figure 2.4):

- **Speech to text.** As the name suggests, it is a service that translates speech into text. Features of this service include:

■ **Real-time speech to text translation.** This feature is used in real-time situations to translate audio streams into text that can be used by applications, tools, and devices.

■ **Batch speech to text.** It allows the asynchronous transcription of large volumes of audio stored in Azure blob storage into text. TO receives asynchronous transcription results; all you need to do is point to the audio files that have a shared access signature. Batch speech-to-text also enables features like sentiment-analysis.

■ **Multi-device conversation.** This feature enables speech to text translation when multiple clients or devices are connected in the same conversation and are sending and receiving audio messages.

■ **Conversation transcription.** Conversation transcription is a solution to provide asynchronous and real-time speech to text conversion by combining speech recognition, speaker identification, and sentence attribution to each speaker. It is also used for in-person meetings and can distinguish among features.

■ **Create custom speech models.** This feature enables you to create and train custom acoustic, language, and pronunciation models using a set of online tools that can evaluate and improve speech to text accuracy in your models.

■ **Text to speech.** As the name indicates, text to speech translates input text into a human-like speech using an XML-based markup language called Speech Synthesis Markup Language (SSML).

■ **Create custom voices.** This feature enables you to create unique custom voices as per your product or brand.

■ **Speech translation.** This feature is useful when your application, tools, or devices need speech to speech or speech to text translation of multiple languages in real time.

■ **Voice assistants.** Voice assistants are used when you want to create a human-like conversational interface in your applications or devices. It enables fast and reliable conversation between a device and assistant that uses either of the two: the Bot Framework's Direct Line Speech channel or the integrated Custom Command.

- **Speaker recognition service.** Apart from fingerprint, voice is also a unique characteristic that distinguishes each human being with others. Speaker recognition service enables you to identify the speakers based on the unique characteristics of their voice. Today the most frequently used information to establish identity is through biometric characteristics such as voice, fingerprint, and face. And this is where feature recognition comes into play. Speaker recognition is divided into two phases:

  1. **Enrollment.** This is a process of recording a speaker's voice and extracting unique and valuable features and characteristics. These characteristics are unique because every human being has a different physical configuration of their vocal track. These features and characteristics are then used to create a voiceprint. Voiceprint is a unique biometric signature and an acoustic frequency spectrum that carries speech information in the form of unidimensional acoustic signals. If we discretize these signals, they can be processed by any conventional computer.

  2. **Recognition.** After creating a unique voiceprint of the speaker, we need something to compare it with. Here comes recognition, a process that compares the sample audio file of the speaker with the voiceprint and identifies the speaker. It offers two services:

     a. **Speaker verification** is a process of verifying input speech with the identity.

     b. **Speaker identification** is a process of identifying the person who is speaking from the group of speakers.

Let's investigate a real-time application of this service. Wouldn't it be easier if instead of using a keyboard to write text documents or fill out forms you could use your voice to convert whatever you say into text?

Dynamics 365 Human Resource management system uses these services for the recruiting process. The recruitment process starts by calling the candidate or emailing the candidate about the open spot in your company. Usually, the first interview is held on a call and if everything goes well the candidate is called for further face-to-face interviews or processes. Previously HR used to type in all the information of the respective candidate manually, including scheduling the interview, but now times have changed. Azure cognitive speech services enable employees using the HR management system to fill out all the candidate-related details such as name, gender, contact number, current salary, current designation, expected salary, expected designation, and so on by using their voice. All this information gets automatically transcribed into the software-separating speaker, which reduces the possibility of manual error and also saves a lot of time.

How does HR benefit from these services?

- Data is fed into the system automatically.
- Speech translation happens despite the language used by the candidate. For example, if the candidate you approached doesn't speak your language, this tool comes in handy. It converts the candidate language into CRM language.
- The text script of the call can be easily mined with the information that could help you to find it in the long term.
- The speech service and the speaker recognition service can support generalized language models so that it can be useful for almost all businesses. But if you want to create a model in any specific language or vocabulary and it is not available in the former services, then custom speech service is used. It is a service that enables you to create your custom models as per your business needs.

Language   Language understanding technology is a machine learning–based service that helps us to correlate between what people say and what they intend. It empowers us to build apps, bots, and IoT devices with a natural language understanding to improve customer experience. For example, if you want to build a general knowledge app and you want it to answer almost all the questions related to all the different subjects like sports, world, entertainment, history, and so on, you can use this language understanding technology to interpret the language of the customer and the meaning of the question he asked. This ability can help your app to predict the accurate answer. Let's assume that the customer asked this question: Who is the greatest badminton player in the world? The answer should be Lee Chong Wei, who holds a total of 55 career titles and is the world's best badminton player (at the time of this writing). Let's look into what services language has to offer (also see Figure 2.5):

- **Bing spell-check.** The Bing spell-check API enables users to correct spelling errors, deliver contextual grammar, and

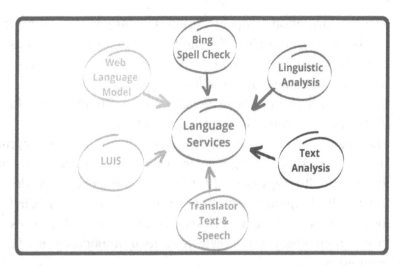

FIGURE 2.5   Language services.

distinguish among names, slang, homophones, and brand names while typing. The Bing spell-checker, instead of relying on dictionary-based rule sets, relies on machine learning and statistical machine translation to produce precisely accurate and contextual corrections.

Features of Bing spell-check include:

- **Multiple spell-check mode.** This mode corrects your grammar and spelling. If we have user input, there is a possibility that it might need some corrections. By adding this feature into your application, you can increase user confidence. It also enables you to produce quality content through your application.

- **Slang and informal language recognition.** Bing spell-check is always updated with the latest expressions and brand names so it can easily identify common phrases and informal terms used in the text.

- **Differentiate between similar words.** Bing spell-check can distinguish between homophones (multiple words that have the same sound but have different meanings and are spelled differently). For example, "pray" and "prey" are words that have the same sound but different meanings and spellings.

- **Brand, title, and popular usage support.** Bing spell-check can identify new brand names, titles, and other common words as they appear.

- **Linguistic analysis.** This API processes language to simplify complex language concepts and to gain access to part-of-speech tagging and parsing text. It is used by businesses to mine customer feedback and interpret user commands.

- **Text analysis.** This API uses advanced natural language processing over untrained data to perform four major functions:

  1. **Sentiment analysis.** This is a very crucial function for your business, as it helps you to identify the sentiment behind the customer's feedback of your brand in discussion forums, customer reviews, social media, and so on. Text analytics API

evaluates the raw text to accurately capture the sentiment behind it. The API returns scores between 0 to 1 where 0 is the most negative sentiment and 1 is the most positive sentiment. For example, if a customer-reviewed your restaurant as "terrible food," then the text analytics API will return 0; however, if a review states that the food is "mouth-watering," then it will return a 1.

2. **Key phrase extraction.** As the name suggests, text analytics API analyzes the unstructured data and returns only the key phrases on it. For example, what if you say the architectural design of the house is awe-inspiring? In this case, the API will return the main points that are enough to understand the meaning of the data such as "architectural design," "house," and "impressive." This function of text analytics API is useful when you have to go through a series of documents in a small amount of time. It will help you to quickly identify the summary of the documents. This feature can be very valuable for law firms.

3. **Language detection.** This feature is used to analyze input text and extract language identifiers for every document such as language used in the input text, dialects, variants, and some regional or cultural languages if used. The text analysis REST API returns a score between 0 and 1, the range for the power of the analysis.

4. **Named entity recognition.** This feature is used to evaluate and categorize your input text such as places, organizations, people, quantities, percentages, date/time, and currencies. The text analytics API extracts the list of non-ambiguous entities and returns web links with more information on these entities.

■ **Translator text and speech.** Translator text API is a cloud-based neural machine translation service that offers statistical machine translation technology and is used to translate text in real-time scenarios. You can integrate this API into your applications that require multi-language support such as messaging applications, e-commerce, website localization, internal communication, and customer support.

▪ **Web language model.** It is a REST API that provides state-of-the-art tools for natural language processing and the power of predictive language models to help us in handling natural language queries.

▪ **Language understanding intelligence services.** Language understanding intelligent service (LUIS) is one of the Azure cognitive services. By using this service, developers can build smart applications that can converse and understand human language and give responses accordingly. LUIS empowers developers to extract useful information from any sentence in the form of "intent," "entity," and "utterances." Even if you have no prior knowledge or understanding of machine learning, you can still build a custom application as per your business needs using LUIS.

Knowledge This is a succession of speech. As through speech, meaning is used to derive knowledge. Knowledge APIs provide ways to map our complex information and data to perform tasks that require intelligence such as semantic search and showing accurate recommendations. Knowledge APIs are divided into six categories (also see Figure 2.6):

1. **Academic knowledge.** Microsoft Academic Knowledge API is a service that serves as a computer administrator to interpret user queries for academic intent and retrieve rich information on topics the user is interested in. It uses Microsoft Academic Graph (MAG) and natural language semantics to retrieve the most relevant entities as per user request.

    Here, Microsoft Academic Graph is a heterogeneous entity graph composed of scientific publication records, reference relationships between those publications, field of study,

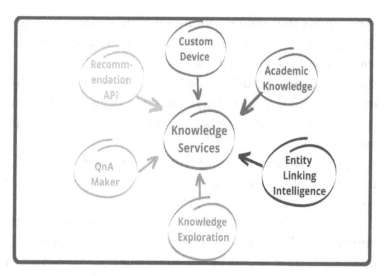

FIGURE 2.6 Knowledge services.

authors, institutions, scholarly papers, journals, conferences, venues, and events. Natural language semantics refers to how users speak or communicate ideas.

2. **Entity linking intelligence service API.** This API is used to identify entities that might be available in the content and link them. The content can be anything such as a news article, a Twitter feed, or a blog post. All we need to do is submit the content to this API and the service will then return the list of entities retrieved from that content.

   For example, in one of the articles, it says: Android Oreo is the fifteenth version and the eighth release of the mobile operating system Android. In this sentence, Android Oreo might be an important entity.

   But then we have another sentence that says: One of the best-selling cookies in the United States is Oreo.

   Both the sentences have the entity Oreo in it, but obviously they are used in different contexts. How does this service do entity linking?

Entity linking is the capability to determine whether the word "Oreo" is being used in the context of Android or as the cookies. The presence of knowledge bases from Wikipedia and Bing enables the entity linking to identify and disambiguate the identity of the entity in the content.

Based on the context of the content, the entity linking intelligence service provides two different concepts: recognition and disambiguation.

- **Entity recognition** refers to identifying entities from an unstructured text despite the entity's existence in the knowledge base.
- **Entity disambiguation** is a task performed to map entities from an input content to the respective unique identities in the target knowledge base. For example, the name of companies, countries, or persons.

3. **Knowledge exploration.** Knowledge Exploration Service (KES) API translates natural language queries and offers an effective and interactive search with auto-completion suggestions and refinement to applications. This API evaluates structural data that is stored in your database and returns information about matched objects. It enables you to build a compressed index from structured data and provides attribute visualizations, interactive query formulation, and faceted experiences.

4. **QnA Maker.** QnA Maker is a service that can efficiently create a conversational application to communicate with the users and answer their questions in natural language. It uses a custom knowledge base to extract the appropriate answer to the user's questions. QnA Maker can be used in social media applications, speech-enabled desktop applications, chatbots, and so on.

The efficiency and accuracy of QnA Maker depend on how well its custom knowledge base is. To create a knowledge base for QnA Maker, you need to import your structured and semi-structured data in the form of question-and-answer sets.

Then the import process extracts the necessary information from structured and semi-structured data to indicate the correlation and dependency between questions and answers sets. Once the knowledge base is ready, you publish it so that users from client applications can ask questions and QnA Maker then processes the question by using the knowledge base to answer the question appropriately.

5. **Recommendations API.** Recommendation API is used by many online businesses to predict customer behavior. It provides direct access to the user's profiles so that your application can predict three kinds of recommendations:

a. Similar items of other brands

b. Frequently bought together items

c. Personalized items (that a user might buy based on previous choices)

Intelligent recommendations can result in increased product sales and personalized customer experience, thus leading to increased revenue. But most online e-commerce businesses don't find it easy to implement recommendation engines. They find it challenging to create sophisticated and fine-tuned algorithms to ensure quality analysis.

Microsoft's cognitive services make it easy for them. They offer a recommendation engine API designed to make recommendations more effortless than ever before. It recommends products based on relevance and based on novelty. For example, for products that are new and not yet encountered by customers, Microsoft has trained its recommendation engine API to emphasize serendipity and diversity. The API uses cognitive computing to produce results like Frequently Bought Together products, customer-to-item flows, and item-to-item recommendations. It also uses Matrix Factorization algorithms to gain insights that insinuate latent features in transactions between users and items. By using this API, businesses can increase sales conversion rates, upsell specific customers using the insights gained, promote the right products based on the demand, and optimize the relationship with the customers.

In fact, the online retailers – for example, DutchCrafters, a Sarasota-based online Amish handmade furniture business – have raised their conversion rate to 0.6 percent by using Microsoft's Recommendation API.

6. **Custom decision service.** As the name suggests, custom decision service is a contextual decision-making API that makes intelligent decisions for you and provides more personalized content to you by analyzing your patterns and learning from it. It uses reinforcement learning to keep up with the emerging trends based on your interests. This API learns and sharpens with experience.

Search Azure Cognitive Search is the only cloud search-as-a-service solution that empowers developers with built-in AI capabilities that can enrich search experiences on all types of information over private, heterogeneous content in mobile, web, and enterprise applications.

The data in the real world is slovenly. It often traverses media types like text documents, PDF files, images, and databases that change invariably, but the valuable knowledge that resides in these data sources is not promptly usable. To retrieve latent knowledge from large data stores is a very challenging task. Businesses use Azure Search in combination with cognitive search capability to accomplish this task.

Let's understand with an example where Azure Search can be used.

Let's assume you have an online e-commerce business. And to provide better usability, it's essential to have search functionality on your website. When customers search for the product, they don't want to waste their time browsing the whole website; by using search functionality they can instantly get what they want. What products customers search for is totally up to them, but what result is to be shown for their query is up to you.

Let's say customers searched for party dresses in your online store and you need to promote a brand, Forever 21, who is paying you to do so. Showing the products of Forever 21 at the top of the search results increases the chance of customers buying those products.

This is one of the scenarios where you can use Azure Search to customize your own search functionality according to your business needs. Moving on to the Azure Search APIs:

- **Bing auto-suggest.** This API is used to enhance the user's search experience in applications by returning all the possible related query suggestions in a drop-down box based on the partial query string in the search box. It is an intelligent API that empowers users to do more in less time.
- **Bing image search.** Bing image search API enables you to add image search options from static and animated images to detailed insights in your applications. This feature in your application will help users to search the web for matching images. This API returns thumbnails, image metadata, full image URLs, publishing website info, and so on as a result. It also provides filtering and sorting features to simplify the image finding process.
- **Bing news search.** The Bing news search API enables you to integrate Bing news in your application. All you must do is search a news-related query, such as queries related to general news, today's top news, news by specific category, and headlines of various categories, and this API will return relevant articles. The result of this API is in the form of article URL, date added, provider info, image of the article, and related news and categories. To find the link to a specific article, this API also provides sorting and filtering options.
- **Bing video search.** This API enables you to add video search features into your application. The search could include trending videos, previews, and other useful metadata. The API results in providing metadata including encoding format, length of the video, view count, information of the creator of the video, and so on.

- **Bing web search.** This API, when called, can return webpages, news, videos, and so on that are indexed by Bing web search API.
- **Bing entity search.** This API returns people, places, things, and local businesses when searched for. For a more engaging user experience, you can use this API in your app. For example, if you have an online food delivery service, you need to tie up with all the restaurants in your city. Therefore, you can use this API to return specific results like if any customer searches any particular restaurant or if he wants to know the restaurants near him.
- **Bing custom search.** This API enables customers to build easy-to-use, ad-free search solutions on their website or applications. The following are the features provided by this API:
  - This API has complete control over various domains, websites, and subsites so that you can build search solutions for any type of industry such as hospitals, retail, and finance.
  - It enables you to upload the domain of your own interest if it's not already available in the batch.
  - It provides an auto-spell check feature to make corrections in the user's query if necessary.
  - It enables you to block, pin promote, or demote any search result.
  - It has Bing's trusted indexing capabilities.

Azure Bot Service

Before jumping to what is Azure Bot Service and how it can help your business, let's find out if your business needs one.

Does your company handle a high volume of service requests such as password reset, fixing the non-working service, and upgrading the service? Does your company maintain multiple call centers to handle questions about the installation of the product, billing, and other technical questions?

If that's the case, then you might use a chatbot to automate customer support for similar queries that would be available 24/7 to satisfy the needs of today's customer base.

What can Azure bot service do for you in these situations?

Azure Bot Service and Bot Framework provide tools such as SDK, templates, and AI services to build, test, deploy, and manage intelligent bots, all in one place. It helps developers to create bots that understand natural language, use speech, and are intelligent enough to handle questions and answers and more.

Bots act like an intelligent robot that can be used to perform simple and repetitive tasks like answering the same set of questions for every customer that uses your product or, if you have a restaurant business, taking dinner reservations. Now let's go through the bot ecosystem from a high level:

- **Microsoft Bot Framework.** It is a collection of SDKs like Node JS, Javascript, and C# that are used by developers to build and develop bots.
- **Bot Framework Emulator.** It is a desktop application that is used by developers to test and debug their bots locally or remotely.
- **Command line interface tools.** It is a cross-platform tool that augments your bots with additional intelligence and more advanced capabilities by allowing you to interact with different libraries, for example, the language understanding service that we have discussed in the previous section of this chapter.
- **Azure Bot Service.** This is a bots infrastructure in which everything operates. You can upload your bot to Azure once it's developed locally and then the bot service enables us to connect, deploy, and manage our bot to one central location.

Azure Machine Learning Service ▦ **65**

Bot service offers five templates to kick-start the process of building bots:

1. **Basic bot.** This template is used to create a bot that responds with a dialog to user input. This bot needs minimum code and files to get started. It can be used to create conversation flow in your bot.
2. **Form bot.** This template creates a bot that collects input through guided conversation. It is designed to collect only a specific amount of information from the user. For example, if you want to order a pizza, then it will ask you the type of flour, type of pizza, what toppings do you want, and more.
3. **Language understanding bot.** This template is used to create bots that can understand user intent. It uses language understanding intelligence service to provide natural language understanding.
4. **Question and answer bot.** This template is used to create a bot that can answer input questions asked by customers related to the service you are providing.
5. **Proactive bot.** This template is used to send proactive messages to your customers that may or may not be related to the prior conversation like reminding them of any event or communicating any information at any specific time.

If these templates do not fit your requirements, then you can also build a custom bot. Azure Bot Service provides various tools during each stage of bot development. Following is the bot designing and building stages (also see Figure 2.7):

■ **Plan.** As we always do before creating any software, we plan. We gather all the requirements and what we want as our end result. Go through the design guidelines already mentioned for a better understanding. Either you can create a simple bot or include advanced capabilities such as natural language, question-answer, and speech.

■ **Build.** In this stage, you can create a conversational interface in any environment or language that can send or receive messages and events. Either you can use the Azure portal or use C#, JavaScript, or Python templates for bot development locally. This stage offers the following features that can be added to your bot:

■ Natural language processing using LUIS.

■ QnA maker to answer questions asked by users.

■ If you are using both of these models, then it offers a dispatch tool to intelligently determine which one will be used when.

■ The bot can contain media attachments such as graphics, menus, and cards using the Add Cards feature.

■ **Test.** This stage allows you to test your bot before publishing it. It allows you to test your bot on the bot framework emulator that can be run locally. It also allows you to test your bot on the web if configured on the Azure portal.

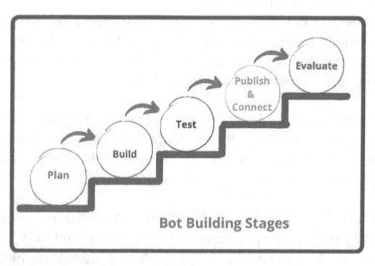

FIGURE 2.7 Bot building stages.

- **Publish.** Once your bot is ready, you can publish it to Azure or your own data center.
- **Connect.** In this stage, you can connect your bot to various channels such as Facebook, Slack, MS Teams, and Telegram. Bot framework sends and receives messages from these platforms, and bot applications receive a unified stream of messages from these channels.
- **Evaluate.** In this stage, the data collected in Azure can be used to enhance capabilities of your bot such as service-level and instrumentation data like latency, integrations, and traffic.

Follow these steps to create a custom bot as per your needs.

KNOWLEDGE MINING

"It's always the hidden insight that's holding you back."

— *Manali Tiwari*

Is your organization one of those whose documents end up hidden away somewhere on a rarely used folder or drive or archive? Are you having trouble in searching and analyzing the data from the documents owned and produced by your organization? It's no surprise that almost 80 percent of organizations fail to explore and understand the content within a limited time constraint. Hundreds of thousands of new documents are generated every day. If every document has something valuable that helps you to unlock opportunities for your organization, then why not do it the right way?

Here comes knowledge mining.

Knowledge mining is all about extracting something useful, profitable, or beneficial from existing information. But there's only so much a mining engineer can do in a significant amount of time. The challenge here is getting full value from the existing data.

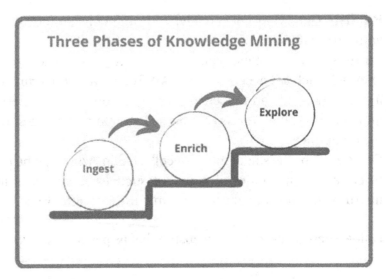

FIGURE 2.8 Three phases of knowledge mining.

This is where knowledge mining using Azure Search comes into play.

Knowledge mining using the cognitive search–based technique can extract valuable information and facts from unstructured data that include PDFs, spreadsheets, images, audio files, and so on.

Using Azure Search in knowledge mining gives you the advantage to bring in a lot of unstructured data with different formats that can be indexed using AI capabilities so that it becomes easily referenceable and searchable.

Note: The data is unstructured if it's not in a database table or in a spreadsheet.

The cognitive search capability in Azure Search enables you to discover patterns in unstructured data and extract meaningful information from it. Knowledge mining using Azure Cognitive Search can be done in three phases (also see Figure 2.8):

1. **Ingest.** Data ingestion process includes loading data documents from various sources to create or update a table in Azure Data Explorer. In Azure Cognitive Search, after the data is ingested, the content loaded in the search index (a persistent storage system of documents used for filtered and full-text search) becomes available to execute queries on it. There are two basic approaches used to populate an index: (1) data is *pushed* into the index programmatically, or (2) point an Azure Cognitive Search indexer (which is a crawler used to extract searchable data from an external Azure data source) at a supported data source. This process is also called a pull model.

   Either pull data from Azure Blob Storage, SQL DB, CosmosDB, MySQL, and Table Storage or push data using APIs to load single or multiple documents into an index. The service renders the unstructured raw data in Blob Storage and derives contents from various file formats such as PDFs and Office documents. It also detects changes through incremental processing, bypassing the hassle to go over the entire data set after initial ingestion.

   Now when we have populated our index, we are overlooked by a refined, responsive UI. The goal of some organizations is achieved in this step, and they stop here since they only want to make their documents searchable.

2. **Enrich.** The data ingested in Azure Cognitive Search is composed of images and other unstructured data sources. Here's where the enrichment capability of Azure Cognitive Search indexing comes to use. It extracts text from unstructured data sources, images, and blobs to make the index and knowledge store more searchable and organized. Built-in cognitive skills in Azure Search enable the implementation of enrichment and extraction processes from data. Some built-in cognitive skills are:
   ■ Natural language processing
      ■ Entity recognition
      ■ Language detection

- ■ Key phrase extraction
- ■ Text manipulation
- ■ Sentiment detection
- ■ PII detection
- ■ Image processing
  - ■ Optical character recognition (OCR)
  - ■ Facial detection
  - ■ Image interpretation
  - ■ Image recognition

These cognitive skills unlock the unstructured raw content and add value in your search or data science apps. This enriched data can be fed to trained models to derive a custom metadata schema. This step, if repeated multiple times, can result in a very powerful and increasingly customized index.

3. **Explore.** Azure Data Explorer is used to query streaming data to help organizations discover insights, identify trends and anomalies, and diagnose problems. Azure Data Explorer provides the following functionality:

   - ■ It helps to pull data from external sources (event hubs) or read ingestion requests from an Azure queue.
   - ■ It makes batches of the data that circulate in the same database and the table to optimize ingestion throughput.
   - ■ It validates data and performs necessary format conversions.
   - ■ It performs all the data manipulation tasks such as organizing, indexing, encoding, compressing data, and matching schema.
   - ■ It manages ingestion load on the engine and handles retries upon transient failures.

At this point, we have a fully populated and meaningful index that is ready to be used by custom applications to provide highly interactive user experiences and rich visualizations.

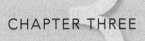

CHAPTER THREE

ML/AI Features and Their Applications in Dynamics 365

TODAY ARTIFICIAL INTELLIGENCE IS transforming how we conduct our work and our lives by offering intelligent solutions to perform our personal and business tasks. It has swiftly taken over all sectors of business.

The Microsoft Dynamics 365 AI is intended to convert your business data into insightful information that can help you to accomplish more from the data and make well-informed business decisions. In this chapter, we will cover how Microsoft Dynamics 365 with ML and AI can improve your business operations.

 ## CUSTOMER INSIGHTS

Do you remember the last time you had a great experience buying any product or using any service? Of course, you do, because that experience made an impression on your memory. And eventually, you became a loyal customer. In today's digital transformation era, organizations are focusing on knowing their customers on a personal level and analyzing their needs and expectations for the improvement of the services or products they are offering. But to know your customers better you should have access to all their data, which is probably dispersed on different systems.

Wouldn't it be easy to have all this data in one place to analyze customer behavior and build a meaningful relationship with your customer by offering what they need and desire? That's the purpose of the customer data platform (CDP).

Microsoft's Dynamics 365 Customer Insights helps you do the same. It helps you to create a 360-degree customer view by connecting data from various transactional, behavioral, and observational sources and harnessing this data to derive intelligent customer insights.

What can organizations achieve by using Dynamics 365 Customer Insights?

- **Data sources.** Organizations can unify customer data from various sources into one place, thus eliminating data silos. Following is the list of data sources or connectors that can be used by an organization to ingest data into Dynamics 365 Customer Insights:
  - **File data sources.** Access, Excel, Folder, JSON, PDF, SharePoint folder, Text/CSV, XML.
  - **Database data sources.** Amazon Redshift, Google BigQuery, IBM Db2 database, Impala, MySQL database, Oracle database, PostgreSQL database, SQL Server database, Sybase database, Teradata database, Vertica.
  - **Power platform data sources.** Dataverse (CDS).

- **Azure data sources.** Azure Blobs, Azure Data Lake Storage Gen2, Azure HDInsight Spark, Azure SQL Data Warehouse, Azure SQL database, Azure Tables.
- **Online services data sources.** Microsoft Exchange Online, Salesforce objects, Salesforce Reports, SharePoint Online list.
- **Other data sources.** Active Directory, OData, Odbc, Share-Point list, Spark, Web API, Web page, Blank table, Blank query.

Bringing together the data generated by diverse sources to provide a complete understanding of business is a very time-consuming and expensive task. So, to resolve this issue, Microsoft and its partners introduced the Common Data Model.

Let's understand what it is with an example: Suppose you have two business apps that were created independently, each having its own different structure and entities (e.g., "consumer" and "lead" are not the same in both the apps). So how is it possible to integrate these two apps with each other? Here comes the Common Data Model, which enables you to build your data in a standardized format so that it becomes easy for the apps to integrate and share data with one another. It provides a set of standard entities attributes and relationships that can be used by all apps to understand, recognize, communicate, and derive insights. Using the Common Data Model as a connector, you can build unified customer profiles. Let's understand step by step how customer insights work:

- **Data unification.** Data unification is a process of creating a single master data set that provides a unified view of your customers. To unify data in Dynamics 365 Customer Insights, you need to follow three steps:
    1. **Map.** Mapping the data in Dynamics 365 Customer Insights is a very important step and consists of two phases:
        a. **Entity selection.** This phase deals with identifying the entities that are associated with customer information, which can be combined to create a dataset.

b. **Attribute selection.** This phase deals with identifying the columns with respect to each entity that you want to consolidate and reconcile in the match and merge steps.

2. **Match.** In this step, you combine the entity datasets created in Map step into a unified customer profile dataset. It should at least have two mapped entities.

3. **Merge.** Merging is the process of resolving the conflicting data that appears in your datasets, for example, if the date format is different in two datasets such as birth date "12/26/94" versus 26/12/94. Merging is done on an attribute-by-attribute basis.

■ **Enriching customer profiles by audience intelligence contained within Microsoft Graph.** Customer profiles can be enriched by connecting Dynamics 365 Customer Insights with Microsoft Graph and Power BI to incorporate audience intelligence and gain a deeper understanding of brand affinity and interests of customers.

Microsoft Graph is a developer's API platform that exposes REST APIs and client libraries to connect to the data residing in Office 365, Windows 10, and Enterprise Mobility and Security services in Microsoft 365, which drives audience intelligence.

Let's understand with an example of what Microsoft Graph can do.

Imagine you are a salesperson at a consumer retail business, and you have the data of approximately 20,000 customers. Wouldn't it be great to know the answers to the following questions:

■ How much might each customer like a competitor's brand that is similar to your own?

■ What are your customer's interests (e.g., sports, movies, or wine)?

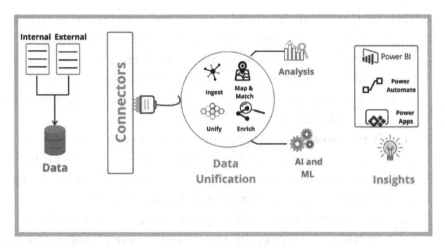

FIGURE 3.1 Artificial intelligence capabilities within Customer Insights.

This data might be available online, not of your customers, of course, but of the people like your customers. To correspond your data with the dataset available online you might have to purchase the data, or the data must be so out of date that it will be of no use for you. Microsoft Graph aids you in this situation by collecting hundreds of millions of data points about the customer and characterizing their behavior by three aspects: age, gender, and location (based on the customer's location). It is done to gain intelligence about brand affinities and interests of customers by comparing your existing customer's data with the interests and brand affinities of people who are similar to them, based on age, gender, and location. After Customer Insights are done with comparison, you can observe the profiles that have been enriched.

- **Activate powerful AI and insights.** AI-enabled Dynamics 365 Customer Insights helps to discover additional business insights with the 360-degree customer view (see Figure 3.1). This unified data is an absolute source to optimize customer engagement and drive personalized customer experiences by building machine learning (ML) models that can generate intelligent insights. Due to Customer Insights' seamless integration with Azure, ML Studio aids in building custom ML models to work on the unified data. This process of building models can be accelerated by using Azure ML Studio–based model pipelines for three frequently encountered use cases:

1. **Churn analysis.** Churn analysis is an evaluation of customers who cease their relationship with a company with the goal of reducing their number. Predicting customer churn can help us retain a current paying customer.

2. **Customer lifetime value prediction.** The customer lifetime value (CLTV) is the key metric to assess and segment each customer's worth. It enables you to improve the experiences and services of high-paying customers. These predictions can help in improving your sales and revenue.

3. **Product recommendations.** This is a personalization strategy used to offer the best services or products to customers based on their attributes, browsing behavior, or situational context, hence, providing a personalized shopping experience.

   Organizations can act and grow their business by using these predictive insights. As stated earlier, they can use Azure Machine Learning to customize and train models that can result in predictive insights. It would be a big help in understanding customer needs so that actions can be taken accordingly.

■ **Empowering business processes by extending Customer Insights with powerful tools and services.** By embedding Customer Insights into business applications such as Dynamics 365 Sales/Marketing/Service or any third-party applications and Power Platform, organizations can do more with their data:

  ■ **Power Apps** helps customers to build custom apps easily and in less time without writing a single line of code. Microsoft Power Apps are built on the foundation of the Common Data

Model and Dataverse that stores the data in a specific format so that developers can use the same data to build and run apps.

- **Power BI** helps in generating additional insights and building reports from unified data. It also enables customizing of reports and dashboards.

- **Power Automate** helps in automating workflows in Dynamics 365 Customer Insights. It enables developers to create workflows in Customer Insights for manual or difficult processes.

Additionally, with Microsoft AI and Machine Learning services, organizations can initiate marketing campaigns by automatically identifying new customer segments and targeting them to improve sales and customer engagement. On the output side, you can bring your audience and segments to Dynamics 365 Marketing.

CUSTOMER SERVICE INSIGHTS

Customer Service Insights is all about improving customer satisfaction by using AI and Machine Learning and building great relationships with your customers. It provides many features and tools to help customer service managers gain a 360-degree view of their customers and performance so that they can implement the best possible solution to resolve the issues occurring while increasing productivity. Let's look into the features that Dynamics 365 Customer Service Insights provides:

- **Omni-channel.** Omni-channel in customer service is a robust application that offers a suite of capabilities that enables organizations to engage with their customers across different digital messaging channels. It also provides a high-productivity, customizable app that can be used by agents to make connections with customers. This app is capable of real-time notification, contextual customer identification, and integrated communication. It also enables managers or supervisors of your organization to use agent productivity tools such as KB integration, search, and case creation to assess real-time operational efficiency of agents.

Dynamics 365 Customer Service Insights offers the following channels:

▩ **Chat.** This channel enables your agents to connect with your customers in real time.

▩ **SMS.** This is an asynchronous mode of communication with your customers that allows your agents to engage with customers through text messages.

▩ **Social media channels.** Dynamics 365 analyzes customer's sentiment and intent in a post that is shared on social channels such as Facebook, LINE, Twitter, and WeChat and automatically converts it into cases.

▩ **IoT sensors.** Dynamics 365 detects the breakdowns in any of your products by watching the readings while they are in use and informing their owners about it.

▩ **Case management.** To understand what the case management feature is, let's first get into what the case is.

The case is a concern or an incident reported by your customers that needs your attention to provide the best possible solution. To find the best possible solution for a case, you need to find the root cause of the problem by tracking the process from the start to assess the intake of the incident and following the remediation process to the final resolution. A case can be anything, for example:

▩ **Questions.** Your customer might have questions regarding your product or service. For example, if a customer is willing to buy a shampoo of your brand and your product description on your website doesn't have the information needed by the customer, naturally the customer will ask the question regarding your product before purchasing it. The question can be anything, such as, is the shampoo good for dry and frizzy hair? Is this shampoo mild? What is the return policy if it doesn't suit me?

■ **Requests.** Customers might have a request that requires a specific action. For example, let's say your product is a house-cleaning tool, a "spin mop cleaning system with one microfiber mop." You are providing only one microfiber mop with the cleaning system and your customer requested you to provide at least two microfiber mops, such that if one gets used up the whole cleaning system is of no use and the customer has no choice other than buying the whole product again.

■ **Issues.** Customers might have a complaint regarding defects in the product or billing issues. For example, your customer ordered a light blue shirt but instead received the same shirt but in navy blue, which is not exactly what he had in mind. So he had no choice other than to complain about this issue.

Customer Service Insights uses natural language understanding to automatically group your cases into topics. These topics are then used to discover problem areas and adapt to current and emerging trends to improve brand sentiment. It's always good to resolve a problem before it gets big, so analyzing and fixing issues before they impact customers will improve customer experience.

Customer Service Insights provides an end-to-end case management solution that recognizes the category of the case and assigns the best-suited agent who can resolve the case efficiently. The following are the components that work together to provide efficient solutions:

■ **Cases.** A case represents anything in the context of a service, such as a customer interaction, that requires a resolution or an answer. A single customer can be associated with multiple resolutions at the same time.

■ **Activities.** An activity involves having a conversation with a customer, like on a phone call. A single case can be associated with multiple activities.

- **Entitlements.** Entitlements represent the number of support services that a customer is empowered with. It's like support contracts.
- **Knowledge articles.** The knowledge base is a repository of informational articles used by customer service representatives to resolve cases.
- **Queues.** A queue is like a waiting area where activities and cases that need processing are organized and stored.
- **Service level agreements (SLAs).** SLAs are like rulebooks that track and define what should happen when a case is opened.
- **Record creation and update rules.** Record creation and update rules are applied to automate the process of record creation and updating in Dynamics 365, depending on the type of the activity.
- **Routing rules.** Routing rules are those rules that automatically route cases to a specific queue or user.
- **Business process flows.** A business process flow is a well-defined process that has various stages and steps to resolve a specific item, like a case.
- **Knowledge management.** The knowledge management module is a collection of knowledge articles that addresses various issues encountered by your customers who are using your product or services. Knowledge articles can be of different types, such as solutions to common issues, frequently asked question documents, and a document with all product information. A knowledge article is like a go-to document for agents because it helps them to find answers to the questions asked by customers. Agents can also email some of these documents to the customers. You can also create and manage your knowledge articles using Dynamics 365's visual editor.
- **Templates.** Dynamics 365 Customer Service Insights provides ready-to-use templates for emails, entitlements, and articles.

So while creating any of these entities, instead of writing them each time, agents can simply use these pre-written templates to save time.

▪ **Dashboards and reports.** Dynamics 365 Customer Service Insights enables you to assess the performance value of your customer service department by using key customer service metrics. These dashboards provide you with reports that have information related to the cases based on their communication channel, agent, or priority. There are different types of dashboards that help you identify areas of improvement in your business by giving you a comprehensive description of your customer service system. This way you can increase customer satisfaction. Let's look in detail at what kind of improvement areas are highlighted by Customer Service Insights:

  ▪ **AI insights charts.** It uses language understanding technology to identify and group support cases in the form of topics so that you have no trouble in classifying the highly impacted positive and negative cases. The following are the charts that show the support cases which have a greater impact on resolution time and customer satisfaction:

    ▪ Customer satisfaction drivers (customer satisfaction dashboard)
    ▪ Resolution time drivers (resolutions dashboard)
    ▪ Top CSAT impactors (topic details dashboard)
    ▪ Top resolve time impactors (topic details dashboard)

  ▪ **Resolution time charts.** It provides you with different views of the time taken to resolve support cases. The following are the charts that provide resolution time:

    ▪ Average resolve time KPI Summary chart (KPI summary dashboard)
    ▪ Unresolved cases by age (KPI summary dashboard)
    ▪ Current popular topics (new cases dashboard)
    ▪ Emerging topics (new cases dashboard)

- ■ Agents with longest resolve time (resolution dashboard)
- ■ New cases versus average resolve time (resolution dashboard)
- ■ New escalations versus resolved escalations (resolution dashboard)
- ■ Resolution time drivers (resolution dashboard)
- ■ Agents with longest average resolve time (topic details dashboard)
- ■ Top CSAT impactors (topic details dashboard)
- ■ Top resolve time impactors (topic details dashboard)
- ■ **Customer satisfaction charts.** It provides different views of customer feedback. The following are the charts that represent customer satisfaction:
  - ■ Average CSAT KPI summary chart (KPI summary dashboard)
  - ■ Popular topics (new cases dashboard)
  - ■ Emerging topics (new cases dashboard)
  - ■ Average CSAT (customer satisfaction dashboard)
  - ■ Customer satisfaction drivers (customer satisfaction dashboard)
  - ■ Average CSAT KPI chart (topic details dashboard)
  - ■ Overall average CSAT impact chart (topic details dashboard)
  - ■ Top CSAT impactors (topic details dashboard)
  - ■ Top resolve time impactors (topic details dashboard)
- ■ **Agent performance chart.** It helps you identify low and high performing support agents. The following are the charts that represent agent performance:
  - ■ Agents with longest average resolve time (case resolution dashboard)
  - ■ Agents with most escalations (case resolution dashboard)
  - ■ Agents with most unresolved cases (topic details dashboard)
  - ■ Agents with longest resolve time (topic details dashboard)
  - ■ Agents with lowest average CSAT (topic details dashboard)
- ■ **Support channel charts.** It is used to identify the performance of systems on different support channels. The following

are the charts that provide different views of support channel performance:

- Case channel (KPI dashboard)
- Case channel (incoming cases dashboard)
- Case timing (incoming cases dashboard)
- Average CSAT (customer satisfaction dashboard)

The customer service insights give you an upper hand in recognizing and understanding customer expectations by giving you a comprehensive view of your customers and performance. You can use it to understand the issues arising and resolve them. It can definitely take your business to the next level.

 ## SALES INSIGHTS

"A great coach is the one who observes your every move and encourages you to become better at what you do."

– Manali Tiwari

Have you ever encountered a situation where your wardrobe is full of clothes and your shoe rack is full of shoes but still you have nothing to wear? More than 20 percent of your wardrobe contains clothes that you wore only once and will not be wearing ever again. This 20 percent of clothes are those that you didn't need to buy in the first place but were compelled by a salesperson to buy them anyway. Well, this is a kind of thing that can ruin your business. Customers don't like to be compelled to purchase anything; instead, they want a salesperson to understand their needs and then suggest the product accordingly. This approach requires a lot of market research, trend analysis, and expertise in that area to suggest the right product to customers. But what if you can get all this in one place? What if there's a way to analyze the conversation styles of each seller so that you can coach them to improve their performance for maximum output?

Dynamics 365 Sales Insights is an application that uses artificial intelligence to generate insights from your customer call data and intelligently couple it with Dynamics 365 to make strategic sales decisions.

What can sales insights do for your business?

- Dynamics 365 Sales Insights helps sales managers to keep up with the latest trends, brands, and competitions by analyzing the calls of customers and understanding their needs and expectations. This data can then be used to train sellers, respectively.
- The Teams overview page of this application enables sales managers to observe the conversation style of the sellers and customer sentiments with respect to each seller. This can help managers to provide personalized coaching to sellers to improve their performance. It can also help managers to track valuable deals and guide the sellers to bring them to a healthy state.
- Sales Insights helps managers to analyze the behavior and patterns of the top sellers of your company and bring those methods in for the rest of the team.
- The seller details page gives you a quick look at sales and conversations. Managers can leave coaching comments against each transcript of the conversation. This page consists of suggested questions that can help managers to undercover trends. Managers can also directly ask questions using the natural conversational language, for example, how many leads are the quality leads? Or how many leads are on the verge of closing?
- Dynamics 365 Sales Insights provides managers with predictive and proactive insights so that they can intelligently help their teams towards achieving greater goals.
- Dynamics 365 Sales Insights helps you to build better business relationships, earn the trust of your customers, engage with the

right buyers, take the right actions based on insights, and make valuable connections. It also helps you to evaluate previous achievements and plan your next moves.

The features of Sales Insights are categorized as follows:

- Free sales insights features
- Advanced sales insights features
- Conversation intelligence

Free Sales Insights Features

As the name suggest, the following features are free with Dynamics 365 Sales:

- Assistant
- Auto capture
- Email engagement

Assistant

Sales Insights Assistant acts like a backbone to support your relationship with customers and prospects. It is just like a personal assistant but better. Sales Insights Assistant can make your life easy and organized in the following ways:

- It monitors your communications and actions with your customers and analyzes this data to generate insights cards. Now let's look into what insights cards are. Insights cards are like an intelligent reminder that uses the data available in Dynamics 365 sales applications and in your inbox and calendar to keep you up to date with your work. For example, it reminds you to send a follow-up email when needed, when to attend a meeting, and so on. Each of these insights cards contains a message that summarizes the content of the card with the set of actions that need to be taken. The assistant also sets the cards by priority and filters them according to your actions.

- It notifies you when an account or contact has been inactive for a while.
- It identifies the emails and conversations that have not been replied to and need attention from your end.
- It also reminds you of the closing date of any opportunity.

The insights cards can be categorized into two categories:

1. **Notifications** represents insights cards that remind you of your present day's upcoming events, meetings, past due items, or events that need your immediate attention.
2. **Insights** cards are the result of the analysis of the data based on AI-driven models to produce intelligent suggestions that may be helpful to sellers in understanding the need of the customer. For example, it can generate a card that highlights an email with a positive sentiment that could become a possible prospect for the seller. However, it can also generate a card for an email highlighting a negative sentiment and warn you that an opportunity can get out of hand if appropriate action is not taken.

Now that we know what an insights card can do for you, let's go through the five elements of a card one by one (also see Figure 3.2):

1. **Main content area** includes the title of the card, summary, card type, as in notification or insights, and other basic information related to the card.
2. **Actions area** is filled with recommendations or actions that should be taken. It generally provides links to make you understand what action can be taken in this situation. The number of links and types may vary from card to card.
3. **Snooze,** like your alarm, works the same way with the cards. It sets the time of snooze to one hour for all the high-priority cards

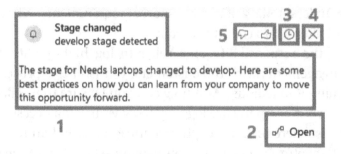

FIGURE 3.2 Five elements of the card.
Source: https://docs.microsoft.com/en-us/dynamics365/ai/sales/assistant

of today and all the low-priority cards can be snoozed for 24 hours. The card will again be visible after the snooze time is over.

4. **Dismiss** can be used if you don't want to perform the actions recommended by any of the insights cards; you can simply dismiss the card permanently.

5. **Feedback** is given about the card, whether it was useful for you or not. This feedback can be seen by Microsoft and your organization managers, so that they can make changes accordingly if needed to improve the results.

So far, we have learned that Assistant is an intelligent tool that can improve the performance of your sales teams using AI-driven models. Who needs a human assistant if this can do wonders for your sales?

We now move on to the next feature, auto capture, which is also free of cost for Dynamics 365 Sales users.

Auto Capture

Data collection is a crucial step for a sales organization, as it helps them have a better understanding of their customers' needs. It can also help them improve in areas like optimizing their marketing strategies and personalizing communication, and can help them gain a deeper understanding of current market requirements. Next, whose responsibility is it to collect this data?

It is the responsibility of a seller to log high-quality data of their engagements with the customers. But isn't this process time-consuming and tedious? And how can you be sure that sellers who work for your company are logging every vital detail necessary?

This is where the auto-capture feature comes in handy.

Auto-capture concentrates on helping sellers log all the crucial customer-related activities in Dynamics 365 Sales Insights by making the process of data entry easy and assuring its completeness. It can automatically add email communications and essential meetings to the organization's timeline of all the concerned records.

It also manages activities and contexts from emails, meetings, and calls and provides suggestions to sellers to save relevant information, for example, creating new contacts. This way, the sellers can spend more time closing the deals than regularly updating the data on Dynamics 365 Sales Insights.

Auto capture feature comes in two categories:

1. **Basic auto capture.** This feature captures the seller's relevant activities and displays it on the Dynamics 365 Sales timeline. If a seller wishes to find all the data related to any particular event in Dynamics 365 Sales, he can get all of it on the timeline (see Figure 3.3). The timeline can show up to 50 recent email suggestions and meetings related to that event. Let's see what this feature can do for you:
   - It detects which emails and meetings are relevant to the current record and then captures them. These emails and meetings are labeled as untracked and are only visible to the seller.
   - Every untracked email has a tracking link (see Figure 3.4). It is only visible to the seller in context. If a seller chooses to select the tracking link, this untracked message gets saved into the Dynamics 365 Sales database, and it will be visible to all the other members of your team as well.

FIGURE 3.3 Timeline of Dynamics 365 Sales.
Source: https://docs.microsoft.com/en-us/dynamics365/ai/sales/free-auto-capture

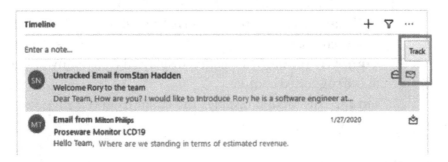

FIGURE 3.4 Untracked email with tracking link on right.
Source: https://docs.microsoft.com/en-us/dynamics365/ai/sales/free-auto-capture

2. **Premium auto capture.** This feature helps the seller to convert a prospect into a customer. It relieves sellers from the trouble of logging every single customer-related detail into Dynamics 365 Sales. Along with all the essential auto capture capabilities, it also provides suggestions to create new contacts. Let's see what this feature can do for you:

■ It displays all the captured activity suggestions on your timeline for you to review and decide which of them are relevant and can be saved for the other team members. Sellers can save, delete, or edit any activity as per their requirement.

- The activity suggestion grid displays all the suggestions captured in one place, ensuring that no information is lost. This section consists of the following columns:
  - **Activity.** This column is concerned with the type of event (i.e., email or meeting).
  - **Sender.** As the name suggests, this column is concerned with the sender of the activity.
  - **Subject.** This column specifies what the activity is about.
  - **Regarding.** This column is concerned with the record with which this activity is associated.
- The contact suggestion captured through the seller conversation is displayed in one place, known as the contact suggestion grid. It consists of the following sections:
  - **Full name.** This section displays the full name of the suggested contact.
  - **Company name.** This section displays the company name of the suggested contact.
  - **Email.** This section displays the email ID of the suggested contact.

Email Engagement

Choosing an effective medium for communication is one of the first steps businesses take to target their audiences. Generally, they go with email communication because it is cheap, fast, and convenient. When you open your email, you see your inbox filled with emails of products and services based on your previous history of purchasing or browsing. But is it the best way of grabbing the customer's attention toward your product or services?

Forty percent of customers don't even bother to open promotional emails. Therefore, how can you be sure that the customer has received the email or if the customer opened the email or not? Can you be sure that your customer understood the intent of the email the way you intended? What if not?

If you don't have answers to all these questions, how will you determine possible prospects that can become customers?

"The only problem with email communication is the uncertainty of knowing."

— *Manali Tiwari*

What if there's a way to have answers to these questions about customers?

Dynamics 365 Sales has made it possible to close more and more deals using email communication. The email engagement feature of Dynamics 365 Sales is like a hawk that keeps an eye on your every email conversation and helps you to be more productive in closing your prospects.

Let's talk about what this email engagement feature of Dynamics 365 Sales can do for you. Today sellers need to understand what customers desire by knowing their interests. The email engagement feature takes you one step closer to closing.

What can this email engagement feature of Dynamics 365 Sales do for you?

Email engagement helps you to track customer activity. For example:

- **You can know when a customer opened your message.** Also, you are alerted when the customer opens your message for the first time. Let's understand how this is possible. When you send an email message to customers using Dynamics 365 Sales, it automatically generates a one-pixel, transparent, invisible, uniquely recognized GIF and attaches it as a linked image with all the other links of your mail. This GIF is one of the first things that is stored in your Dynamics 365 server along with other images, and it gets loaded only when the receiver chooses to download all the images. When the receiver requests to download a unique GIF, then your Dynamics 365 Sales designates that the associated message was opened and records the device type. Thus, if you want to know that the customer opened your message or not, you have to attach lots of compelling images with the mail so that when a customer downloads the image, it gets loaded, and you will know.

■ **You can know when each link of the mail was clicked.** Let's understand how. When you send a follow-up email to your customer, all the hyperlinks of your message are automatically converted to unique redirect links that point to the Dynamics 365 server. Every redirect link consists of an ID that uniquely represents the message and the URL of the initial target link. When the customer clicks on the link, a request is sent to the Dynamics 365 server, which logs the click and then redirects it to its original address so that the receiver still gets all the information needed with little or no delay.

■ **You can know when the receiver opened each attachment.** Let's understand how. When you add a followed attachment in your email, it is added as a link and stored on the OneDrive for Business share used by your Dynamics 365 server. And if we talk about unfollowed links, when a receiver downloads the attachment, the Dynamics 365 server notes the click and the time.

■ **Based on the customer's email opening history, it helps you to schedule the most effective time to deliver your message, taking into consideration the recipient's time zone.**

■ **It recommends several email templates based on the previous conversation history with the customer.** You can choose the most appropriate one and send it.

■ **You can set a reminder that can alert you to send follow-up emails.** It uses the assistant feature to deliver alerts and other messages, so it is essential to enable this feature to take full use of the email engagement feature.

The email engagement feature can take your business to new heights by helping you to create useful email messages and understand your customers' needs so that you can approach them with a solution.

Until now, we have covered all the free features of Dynamics 365 Sales. Let's move on to some advanced and premium features and see what it can do for your business.

Advanced Sales Insights Features

The advanced sales insights features have it all. It has all the free features along with the following more exciting and more prolific features:

- **Assistant with studio.** It consists of all the capabilities mentioned above for the free version and some enhanced capabilities such as:
  - You can create and display custom insights cards using the studio through Microsoft Flow.
  - You can prioritize cards according to your needs.
  - You can optimize card ranking.
  - You can assign cards to your team members respective of their roles.
  - You can turn on or off insights cards, enabling you to display cards according to specific user roles.
  - You can edit the overall flow of an insights card.
- **Relationship analytics.** This is a feature that uses a database to create a graphical representation of key performance indicators for any lead, contacts, account, or opportunity.
- **Predictive lead scoring.** This feature creates a scoring model for all the leads available in your pipeline and identifies and prioritizes quality leads and converts them into opportunities.

- **Predictive opportunity scoring.** The scoring model also helps you to prioritize opportunities as well.
- **Premium forecasting.** This feature uses AI-driven models to analyze revenue outcomes based on historical data and enables the sales team to focus on opportunities with a high-revenue generation score.
- **Notes analysis.** This feature analyzes the notes taken by your sellers while conversing with the customers and guides them intelligently until the end of the process.
- **Talking points.** It enables your sales teams to initiate the conversation with the customers by suggesting some common conversational topics such as family, sports, and entertainment.
- **Who knows whom.** This feature provides information about the customers' mutual contacts if any of your colleagues is a friend of the customer. It can help you to get introduced to a possible prospect.
- **Sales accelerator.** It accelerates the process of searching the next best possible lead. It gathers information from multiple sources and creates a prioritized and robust pipeline that enables sellers to approach the lead intelligently.
- **Dynamics 365 Assistant for teams.** It provides sellers with intelligent guidance, so that they can build a meaningful relationship with their customers. This application enables sellers to be prepared for the upcoming engagements and events of the day, helps them prepare for meetings, suggests the next best action intelligently, captures meeting notes, and scans business cards to create new contacts.

Conversation Intelligence

Conversation intelligence enables the sales manager to coach sales teams to proactively explain the business to customers and answer the questions related to the business.

 **PRODUCT INSIGHTS**

For businesses, it is essential to know how well people are responding to your product: Which features are most used by customers, and which are pretty much ignored? Product insights are an intelligent way to get real-time insights into your product while customers are using them. You can improve and support like never before. For example, let's say your product is air conditioners. Dynamics 365 Product Insights can help you gather all the data around energy consumption, refrigerant level, outdoor condenser coils, and indoor evaporator units from every air conditioner you sold. It then combines that data to your Dynamics 365 applications like PLM, ERP, CRM, and other systems to give better visibility of how customers use your product. Gathering this crucial data can help you improve your future releases, enable you to proactively provide customer service, and help you to develop new features according to customer needs for better customer experiences.

Benefits of product insights include:

- **Improve your product.** Product insights help you improve the quality of the product and customer experience by monitoring its usage.
- **Product planning.** Product insights help you identify the needs of customers using data to plan your future releases accordingly. It enables you to engage directly with customers for ideas and feedback.
- **Market value.** Product insights help you to discover how popular your product is. It helps you to figure out the appreciative and non-appreciative features of your product.
- **Proactive servicing.** Product insights use telemetry to identify problems in products/services and warn you to prioritize repairs or design fixes and maintenance.

VIRTUAL AGENT FOR CUSTOMER SERVICE IN DYNAMICS 365

How well your customer service teams manage customer inquiries decides the future of your brand. Today, customers don't want to waste their time connecting to human agents. They want an immediate and intelligent response to all their problems, whether they connect you through call, text, or online. But it is becoming impossible for companies to provide a personal experience to every customer as needed, so companies are turning toward virtual agents to manage many inquiries.

Let's understand how Dynamics 365 Customer Service Insights and virtual agents enable teams to provide a personalized experience to all customers and anticipate their needs without writing a single line of code.

In Dynamics 365 Customer Service Insights, the data from thousands of calls across multiple channels is collected and displayed in the key performance indicator summary dashboard. It uses AI to show you emerging topics through a variety of charts, providing you with a graphical representation of your system's key performance indicators. Let's take one of the charts to understand how virtual agents can help: a case volume driver chart. This chart groups all the support cases as support topics using AI clustering based on deep learning and natural language semantics. Due to these charts, teams don't have to review each case individually; instead, the AI algorithm identifies and groups each case with similar intent without actual manual intervention. Let's take one of the cases from the chart that has raised inquiries from many customers. Suppose the customers face challenges printing on a smart printer, and that smart printer is your product. Now, how can you deal with more than 2,000 inquiries a day? This is where you can create a virtual agent to help you provide a personalized experience to each customer without writing code. Steps to create a virtual agent are:

1. Sign up Dynamics 365 virtual agent for customer service.
2. Get the license for Dynamics 365 virtual agent application.
3. Go to https://va.ai.dynamics.com to create a new bot.
4. To create a bot, you need to enter the name of the bot and the environment.
5. The bot has some default topics, but you can create your topic as well. The topic is where you have to specify the bot's actions when the user asks different questions.
6. In this case, let's create a topic named printer troubleshooter. In this topic, you will specify trigger phrases that customers might ask, such as my printer needs to be fixed, it doesn't work, I need to repair my printer, or I need help with my printer. What's interesting is the customer doesn't need to type the exact phrase specified in our topic. Through natural language understanding, the virtual agent is intelligent enough to understand its semantic meaning and intent to make a perfect match.
7. The next step is to edit the conversation to specify the bot's responses to various customer questions. When a customer says that the printer is not working, you can configure your bot to reply as follows: Are you using a smart printer?
8. Now there can be two responses: yes or no. If the user says yes, then your bot should redirect the customer to a smart printer troubleshooter, and if the answer is no, then you can redirect the customer back to the generic topic from where we started.
9. This way, a tree is forming to help you follow where your conversation is heading.

In this process, if you ask the customer for their email address, the virtual agent gets tied in Microsoft Flow, enabling you to get data from Dataverse (CDS), CRM, and other databases. Through the customer's email address, a virtual agent can identify the exact device, the purchasing date, and the serial number. By knowing the exact device, a virtual agent can look into the exact issue the customer is facing and can help in resolving it. It also provides information about any upcoming offers or opportunities related to the product.

A virtual agent for customer service app can help your teams build bots without any coding expertise and easily automate support for common inquiries, thus improving customer satisfaction.

Fraud Protection

In this digital era, more people are flocking to the internet to shop online from the comfort of their homes without worrying about the long queues at the checkout. With the increase in online business sales, a large amount of personal information, including card information, is transferred online, which has made it easier for hackers to access this information and perform malicious activities. Due to this, e-commerce businesses are losing over $250 billion a year on fraudulent transactions. Now, what can we do to protect the revenue and stop these fraudulent transactions?

Dynamics 365 Fraud Protection is an application that helps merchants protect their revenue by decreasing the number of fraud transactions, increasing the acceptance rate, and reducing operational expenses. Let's look into the three capabilities it has to offer:

Purchase protection. It is a cloud-based solution that focuses on improving e-commerce transaction acceptance rates by reducing checkout friction. It uses adaptive artificial intelligence to gather insights that make it easy for merchants to make decisions that include revenue balancing opportunities, customer experience, and fraud loss. This technology continuously learns from the previous data patterns to improve fraud detection accuracy. It also uses a transaction acceptance booster tool that shares transactional trust knowledge with partner banks to boost your authorization rates. This way, it protects your revenue by reducing wrongful dismissal of the payment and increasing acceptance rates. An increase in acceptance rates automatically results in a decrease in operational cost, as now there is no need for manual reviewing.

Account protection. This capability of fraud protection focuses on safeguarding user accounts from abuse and fraud by contending fake account creation or account hacking or unauthorized account access. Adaptive artificial intelligence sets fraud assessment checks on all the critical steps of the account creation process. It provides device fingerprinting capability to boost fraud detection, empowering your team to reduce friction from CAPTCHAs for two-factor authorization. It enables merchants to block fraudulent activity before damage is done. Due to this, merchants can avoid incurring losses by protecting their customers against automated attacks, thus guarding their accounts against fraud and ill usage. This capability improves the merchant's reputation, which strengthens the customer's trust in your business.

Loss prevention. This capability focuses on protecting the business's profits by identifying fraudulent returns and discounts abuse arising from omni-channel purchases. It analyzes fraudulent patterns from omni-channels to capture anomalies and learn from evolving patterns. Based on this, it provides intelligent reports to merchants to increase their attention to potentially fraudulent activity. It works together with a fraud protection network to provide insights through feature calculation, evaluation, and model training. It then equips merchants with the tools they need to mitigate losses and optimize fraud detection related to discounts and returns.

Dynamics 365 Fraud Protection is the best tool to keep your e-commerce business buzzing.

ARTIFICIAL INTELLIGENCE IN POWER APPS WITH AI BUILDER

As we have already learned in Chapter 1, AI builder is a new capability of Power Platform that enables you to add artificial intelligence to your applications and automate processes, and to tailor your AI solution. Power Apps empowers employees to create applications for your business, even if you don't have any prior coding experience. Now, the question is, what can AI Builder do for Power Apps?

AI Builder is a tool that brings the power of artificial intelligence through point and clicks experience and is directly integrated with Power Automate and Power Apps. Developers can build AI models using AI Builder, which uses the data that is already stored in Dataverse, a data store for enterprises. Some capabilities of AI Builder are:

- **Binary classification.** Binary classification is an AI model that uses historical data to predict yes/no business outcomes by analyzing patterns in your historical data. Based on the results, it then understands what factors influence the outcomes, and then it learns the nature of these factors to predict future outcomes. The ability to predict outcomes empowers you to make critical business decisions quickly and grow faster in this competitive era.
- **Text classification.** The AI Builder text classification model can be used to automate business processes and empower your employees to act on the insights. For example, if you work in the hospital industry, what can be done to improve customer service and health care? The hospital industry handles a large amount of data that is ever increasing in nature, so it becomes a challenge to identify actionable insights. To increase customer satisfaction and the hospital's processing efficiency, you can automate some processes, for example, taking feedback from customers. All the data collected as feedback from the customers is stored in Dataverse (CDS). The text classification AI model will then classify, categorize, and group text to recognize sentiments of the feedback and use it to drive workflows. There are four types of text-based classification models:
    1. **Sentiment analysis model.** This model analyzes positive and negative sentiments from the text data. It can be

used to analyze social media posts or customer reviews to name a few.

2. **Entity extraction.** This model identifies the useful data from the unstructured data and classifies it into predefined categories. It can be used to extract facts and retrieve valuable information from the large volume of data.

3. **Key phrase extraction.** This model can extract key phrases from the given text document. For example, if the input text is "It was a great movie, and the popcorn we ate was very delicious," the model will extract "great movie" and "delicious popcorn."

4. **Language detection.** As the name suggests, this model detects the predominant language used in the text document. For example, "I have a cat." For this input text, the model will return "en" as in the English language.

■ **Object detection.** This model lets you count, locate, and identify selected objects from pictures you take with the camera. You can use this model in the retail industry to manage inventory.

■ **Forms processing.** This AI model can automatically extract the essential information from important documents like invoices that are received as PDF email attachments. It can extract address, invoice number, product items, quantity, and rate. After extracting the key elements from the form, it stores the data in Dataverse (CDS). By using this model, you can reduce the possibility of mistakes in manually entering this data.

So, now we have a clear idea of how Power Apps can help organizations build connected apps and automate tasks (Figure 3.5). At the same time, AI Builder enables them to use machine learning and Azure-based cognitive services without the need to write code. By direct, step-by-step guidance via a Wizard, you can bring AI very fast on your own Dataverse and Power Platform environment.

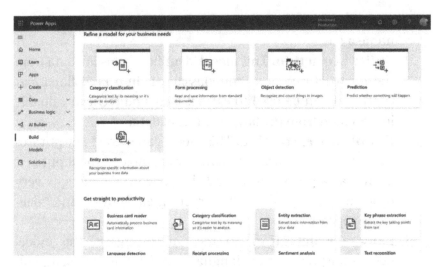

FIGURE 3.5 How Power Apps can help organizations.

  WHAT IS MIXED REALITY?

Mixed Reality is a recent innovation that enables you to manipulate existing environments or create a new one.

> Mixed Reality is like a merger of the real and virtual worlds. It produces an environment where physical and digital objects coexist and interact with each other.

Dynamics 365 Apps for Mixed Reality

Employees are the ones who can take the business to new heights. It's their imagination, capability, resourcefulness, and drive that get the job done. What if there was a way for employees to work together from anywhere when there is a critical issue on their hands? Sometimes even the most skilled employees need help from the experts. Experts may not be with them all the time.

FIGURE 3.6   Mixed Reality component.
Source: https://docs.microsoft.com/en-us/powerapps/maker/canvas-apps/
mixed-reality-overview

Dynamics 365 apps for Mixed Reality empower employees to work side by side with experts from remote locations by sharing what they see. Experts can then guide the on-site employees through the step-by-step process to solve the issues in real time. This new vision of work enables employees to work intelligently by bringing the experts they need with just a tap. They together can troubleshoot the problem and address the issue in less time. This collaboration for problem solving makes your employees more connected, more efficient, and more informed. Power Apps now includes a Mixed Reality component (see Figure 3.6).

Microsoft Hololens

Microsoft Hololens is the world's first unearthed holographic computer that takes on Mixed Reality.

To understand Hololens you need to know the meaning of hologram. Holograms are the objects that appear around you as real objects and are made up of sound and light. You can interact with these objects in the real world through voice commands, gestures, and gaze.

What Hololens does is enables you to create holograms or objects that become part of your physical environment. Hololens consists of multiple sensors, advanced optics, and holographic processing, which are used to create holograms that seamlessly blend with your environment.

Dynamics 365 Mixed Reality Apps

Dynamics 365 Mixed Reality apps need Hololens in a tangible way, as it has several optical sensors to understand the environment and sense it. It has a main camera pointing downward that picks up on hand motions and a techno-specific speaker that accumulates sound from all over the room. The Hololens also consists of multiple microphones, one ambient light sensor, one HD camera, and Microsoft's custom Holographic Processing Unit that contains more processing power than the average laptop. Having all of this together in one device makes Hololens compatible with the spatial bearings of the unit in the room, able to track walls and objects in the room, and able to incorporate holograms into the environment.

Dynamics 365 Remote Assist

The Dynamics 365 Remote Assist application empowers employees to connect with both customers and on-site technicians to solve issues occurring in real time. The application uses Hololens to make and receive video calls. Hololens uses an augmented reality interface and voice commands to connect with the customers; this way, employees don't have to hold any device in their hands. Employees of either side can create or interact with the AR content that is visible through a Hololens wearer's space. The off-site employee can easily visualize what the Hololens wearer is seeing. The Hololens wearer can point out the problem area by creating a circle or arrow around it, which will then become a hologram object. The off-site employee will troubleshoot the problem around this object and can offer guidance step by step to resolve the issue. This is how Dynamics 365 Remote Assist efficiently solves problems in real time with the help of employees available on the remote locations.

Dynamics 365 Guides

The major challenge businesses are facing today is the lack of experience of new employees. Training people requires experts to guide them all the way through the work process and prepare them for all scenarios. But it's not as effective as it needs to be because experienced people are retiring every day. So what can be done for new employees, so that they can work as efficiently as experienced people? With this concept in mind, Microsoft introduced Dynamics 365 Guides.

Dynamics 365 Guides, as the name suggests, is a Mixed Reality learning app with the simple step-by-step instructions written on your system. Businesses provide new employees with the Hololens, which can be used to pick holographic parts, text, diagrams, 3D visuals, and icons that can be placed on an actual machine for learning, to prepare them for real-world situations without the risk or the expense of having them work with actual assets. It helps new employees to get the job done from the very first day. This application enables new employees to work with existing processes with the right guide. The step-by-step instructions move with employees, pointing to the exact tools and parts they need and where they should apply them. What's a better way of learning than practically performing tasks without any risk factor involved? This way, employees can learn faster with fewer errors and more confidence without having to rely on other employees to teach them every step. The app also provides managers a report on how well the new employee has been working and learning. Employees make continuous improvement by adapting faster and becoming more adept at supporting complex aspects of the business, making them more valuable and competitive.

These Mixed Reality applications can make a difference in various industries like automotive, manufacturing, sales, energy, and more by enhancing customer experiences, encouraging employees to be more productive, and helping businesses to reduce costs.

CHAPTER FOUR

Dynamics 365 and Custom ML Models Using Azure ML

"It's the choices you make that determine your future."

– Donny Ingram

WITH INNOVATIONS IN MACHINE intelligence making ML capable of delivering– and sometimes exceeding – human-level performance in perceptual and cognitive tasks, organizations are increasingly evaluating how artificial intelligence can be applied to derive new business value and change the world for the better. It is fair to assume that soon the companies that are using the technologies to automate all the regular and routine work will progress faster than those that aren't.

Technologies like artificial intelligence are transforming the way businesses are operating these days. It is the most trending technology of today and along with Azure cloud-based services, it's doing miracles for organizations small and large, at scale.

■ AZURE MACHINE LEARNING

Azure Machine Learning is a cloud-based environment that:

- Enables you to use cloud-based storage services such as Azure Blob, Azure Data Lake (including Gen2), Azure SQL Database, Azure Synapse Analytics (Modern Data warehouse), PostgreSQL, Databricks, and MySQL. Datasets can also be created from local files, public URLs, or Azure Open Datasets.
- Provides a managed cloud-based workstation optimized for your machine learning development environment called Azure Compute Instances. For more demanding or production grade model training, you can use an Azure Machine Learning compute cluster for additional capabilities.
- Allows you to designate a compute target, which is a designated compute resource or environment where you run your training script or host your service deployment. You can deploy these compute targets as a web service to call for real-time inference, periodically as a batch service, or deployed to an IoT device via a Docker container by using Azure IoT Edge.
- Adds flexibility to build and train models in authoring experiences such as Automated ML, or a visual drag-and-drop Designer, or code-first Notebooks with built-in support for open-source tools and frameworks, IDEs like Jupyter and command-line interfaces, or languages such as Python or R.
- Is a pay-per-use facility, which means you only have to pay for the services you use.

Azure ML can optimize business processes because it:

- **Accelerates the end-to-end machine learning cycle.** Azure ML services enable users to recognize the ideal algorithm by taking advantage of automated tools that aid in building predictive models faster, consuming less time.

- **Supports multiple frameworks.** Azure ML allows users to choose from a variety of frameworks to create AI models. Some of them are scikit-learn, PyTorch, MXNet, TensorFlow, Chainer, and Keras.
- **Offers skill independent experience.** Users can build models using a no-code designer, the Python SDK, Jupyter notebooks, VS Code, or their favorite IDE based on the skill level they possess or the authoring experience they prefer.
- **Uses MLOps for communication between data scientists and the operations team.** It is used to automate plenty of processes and produce more valuable insights by eliminating waste.
- **Is compatible with container orchestration services.** ML services are compatible with Docker, Azure Kubernetes Service, and Azure Container Instances, so it's easy to deploy models to platforms that support the most mission-critical workloads.

As of now, we have determined why Azure Machine Learning solutions are important for business growth. Let's learn about some concepts of Azure Machine Learning.

Many organizations are taking the first step toward implementing machine learning into their business practices. But they face some potential challenges like difficulty in collecting scattered data that lies all over the organization and difficulty in accessing it from wherever you desire. To overcome these hurdles, businesses need to deploy new machine learning models that could take months of engineering investments. Besides that, implementing machine learning in your business flow requires thorough training and the expertise of data specialists to scale, manage, and monitor machine learning systems.

So, to solve these problems, Microsoft combined machine learning with cloud computing and created a machine learning solution called Microsoft Azure Machine Learning. Azure Machine Learning empowers businesses with the add-on benefit of the cloud to build data-driven applications that can predict, forecast, and enhance several business processes.

Azure Machine Learning Concepts

- **Models.** A model is a piece of code that is trained to identify specific patterns from the input and produce output. To create a model, you need to select an algorithm, provide it with data, and tune hyperparameters. It is basically a representation of what was learned by the machine learning algorithm. Once your model is created, you can use the selected algorithm to learn from the set of data. For example, creating a model that can recognize users' facial expressions and identify human emotions requires supervised learning. In this case, you need to train your model by providing example images with different facial expressions, each manually tagged with a specific emotion for it to learn from these images. This is how supervised learning models identify specific patterns from the input data that you provide.

  There are some popular machine learning frameworks that you can use to create a model, such as scikit-learn, XGBoost, PyTorch, TensorFlow, and Chainer.

- **Datasets.** Datasets are the assets in your machine learning workspace that help you connect the data and your storage service to make it available for machine learning experiments. When you create a dataset, you create a reference to your storage service data that enables you to access data through datasets. This way, you can only register your data once and reuse it whenever you want, even for different experiments. Datasets can be used as a direct input for your scripts, Azure Machine Learning pipelines, and Bayesian machine learning. Due to the creation of datasets, data remains in its existing data source location, so there is no extra storage cost, and the integrity of your data sources are not at risk. There are two types of datasets that can be used in Azure

Machine Learning training workflows concerning Automated ML, estimators, hyperdrive, and pipelines:

1. **FileDataset** references single or multiple files in your datastores or public URLs to use in Azure Machine Learning. If the data you want to use is already cleansed and ready for training experiments, then you can use a FileDataset.

2. **TabularDataset** represents data in a tabular format and can materialize the data into pandas or Spark DataFrame to enable you to work with standard data preparation and training libraries.

- **Datastores.** Datastores is a data management capability implemented by the Azure Machine Learning Service that acts as an interface to connect numerous Azure storage services without jeopardizing your data source's integrity. It contains connection information in your Key Vault, including your subscription ID and token authorization, so there is no need to hard code them in your scripts. To create and register datastores, you can use the Azure Machine Learning Studio or the Azure Machine Learning Python SDK.

- **Compute resources.** Compute resource is an environment you can use to host your service deployment or run your script. It can also be used as your local machine or as a cloud-based computing resource. If you use it, you don't have to worry about changing the code when you later shift to a different computing environment. Azure Machine Learning introduces two virtual machines (VMs):

1. **Compute instance.** A virtual machine primarily used in your development workstation, as it consists of multiple machine learning environments and tools. It provides the ability to start running sample notebooks with no setup required. It can also be used as a compute target for training and inferencing jobs.

2. **Compute clusters.** Computer clusters are clusters of virtual machines with multi-node scaling capabilities. They are better used in compute targets for large jobs and production. It scales up automatically when a job is submitted.

When you develop a model, you start by utilizing a small amount of data. So, use your local computer or cloud-based virtual machine as a compute target at this stage. But as you level up to more extensive data or if you want to perform distributed training on your data, you need to use Azure Machine Learning compute to create a single- or multi-node cluster that auto-scales each time you submit a run. Azure Machine Learning compute cluster can be used as a training compute target for most jobs in the Designer authoring experience.

- **Experiments.** An experiment is a run or a group of runs of a specified script belonging to a workspace. It consists of some characteristics that you connect together to construct a predictive analysis model. Characteristics that a valid experiment should have are:
  - It should have at least one dataset and one module.
  - Datasets can only be connected to modules.
  - Modules are connected to either datasets or other modules.
  - All the module's input ports need to have a connection to the data flow.
  - Parameters must be set for each module.
  - Run logs.
- **Pipelines.** Azure Machine Learning pipeline is an autonomously executable workflow of a whole machine learning task. Subtasks in the pipeline are encapsulated as a series of steps. These pipelines can do just about anything from making a call for Python script to more complex tasks. Your pipelines should majorly concentrate on machine learning tasks such as:
  - Importing, cleaning, validating data and transformation, normalization, and staging as done in the data preparation process.

- Training configuration including logging/reporting configurations and parameterizing arguments and file paths.
- Training and verifying the results efficiently and repeatedly. High-level performance can be achieved by specifying specific data subsets, distributed processing, different hardware compute resources, and progress monitoring.
- Deployment tasks that include versioning, provisioning, scaling, and access control.

To create pipelines, Designer enables you to drag-and-drop datasets and modules onto an interactive canvas. The inputs and outputs of every step are displayed visibly. The drag-and-drop feature to create data connections empowers you to understand and alter your pipeline's data flow instantly. When you run the pipeline object, the service performs the following tasks:

1. Calculate the requirements for each step:
   a. Hardware compute resources
   b. OS resources (like Docker image(s))
   c. Software resources (like Conda/virtual env dependencies)
   d. Data inputs
2. It determines the dependencies between various steps, which results in a dynamic execution graph.
3. When each node in the execution graph runs, the following occurs:
   a. The service conceivably reuses existing resources to configure the necessary hardware and software environment.
   b. The step runs and provides logging and monitoring information to its containing experiment object.
   c. Every step's output is treated as inputs to the next step and/or written to storage.
   d. Resources that are of no use are concluded and disconnected.
      The benefits of using pipelines in ML workflow include:
      - It enables you to run steps, either in parallel or sequentially in a reliable and unattended manner.

- You can create multiple pipelines and reliably coordinate heterogeneous compute. This means you can use available compute resources by running individual pipeline steps on various compute targets, such as HDInsight, GPU Data Science VMs, and Databricks.
- Pipelines can be reused by creating pipeline templates for explicit scenarios, like retraining and batch-scoring. You can trigger published pipelines from external systems through simple REST calls.
- For tracking and versioning your data sources, inputs, and outputs, you can use pipelines SDK.
- Pipelines allow multiple data scientists to work on steps across all areas of the machine learning design process.

Azure ML pipeline is a compelling resource that begins with providing value in the early developing stages. Its value rises as the team and projects progress. Azure Machine Learning pipelines are designed to help you build, optimize, and manage machine learning workflows.

- **Pipeline Endpoints.** Pipeline Endpoints is a REST API that can be used from external applications. It enables you to call your ML pipelines via a REST endpoint programmatically and helps you to automate your pipeline workflows.
- **Run logs.** The single execution of your training script is called Run. Azure Machine Learning keeps track of all the runs by storing critical information in the experiment such as:
  - Output files that are either explicitly uploaded by you or are auto collected by the experiment.
  - Metrics.
  - Metadata like timestamp, duration, and so on.
  - A snapshot of the directory that consists of scripts before running the experiment.

To log arbitrary metrics, you can use the Python SDK.

AZURE MACHINE LEARNING STUDIO

Azure Machine Learning Studio is a web-based integrated development environment (IDE) that is closely intermingled with other Azure cloud services to simplify the development and deployment of machine learning models and services. In today's era, businesses use machine learning to achieve predictive intelligence and stay competitive. Still, data scientists and data engineers of many companies find it challenging to adopt machine learning solutions for tedious tasks because it requires slow training and complex deployment.

Microsoft's Azure Machine learning removes these barriers. It is an open platform with automated ML and built-in DevOps that can be used to unlock insights anywhere and accelerate ML lifecycle end-to-end. You can swiftly use it to scale from cloud to edge.

Azure Machine Learning Studio is a powerful drag and drop interface that enables you to start without coding. Just a few clicks can move you from idea to deployment without any additional setup required.

With Automated Machine Learning, you can automate your manual and repetitive tasks, and within no time, you can develop a more innovative model prototype and development. Automated ML is also responsible for intensive feature engineering, algorithm selection, and hyperparameter tuning.

Azure Machine Learning provides out-of-the-box support for many open-source frameworks like ONNX, PyTorch, scikit-learn, TensorFlow, and compatibility for Notebooks-integrated environments and Command line interfaces. It allows you to stick with the technologies you already know and empowers you to use your own set of Python or R tools.

You can use Azure ML Studio to build pipelines that will help you share your end-to-end data science experience and optimize workflows easily. The built-in DevOps can speed up solution deployment and boost productivity. It can help you ensure your model's quality and automatically improve it over time with integrated CI/CD. Using Azure ML Studio can help your team to innovate freely with a model interpretability feature, auto scale compute. It also enables deeper integration with other Microsoft software like Power BI Excel, SQL server, which can help you to take your results to the next level without any hurdles.

To build custom machine learning models, it is crucial to have an experienced team of data scientists and mathematicians who can build, test, and validate models. But it is not easy to find machine learning expertise today. So, what can be done to make the custom model building process easy for everyone?

Businesses need tools to guide developers through the whole process of creating the models that they need. The majority of machine learning models fall into two categories: the one that classifies similar data, and the other that identifies outlying data. So, to empower developers to create custom models, Azure provides pre-trained, pre-built, customizable models along with the various tools that make their task easy.

Authoring Experience in Azure ML Studio

Automated machine learning (Automated ML) is the process of automating the time-consuming, iterative tasks of machine learning model development. More specifically, it automates data preparation, model selection, composition, and parameterization of machine learning models. Automated ML makes machine learning tasks accessible to all users, regardless of skill level, and often provides faster, more accurate outputs than hand-coded algorithms and avoids manual hyperparameter tuning. It enables you to build ML models with high scale, efficiency, and productivity while sustaining model quality using a target metric you specify.

Certain approaches to model development sometimes make these systems hard to explain, meaning it is difficult to understand why AI systems make decisions. Although they produce results with absolute efficiency and processing power, it can be challenging to track how the algorithm produced that output. Consequently, it becomes difficult for us to determine the accurate model for a given problem because it then becomes difficult to predict a result if a model is a black box.

So, in this case, what Automated ML does is, it makes machine learning more accessible, thus making it less of a black box. Automated ML automates parts of the machine learning process that apply the algorithm to real-world scenarios. It learns and understands the algorithm's internal logic and makes choices according to how it relates to the real-world scenarios. When done using Automated ML, the task takes less time and resources and is performed with ultimate efficiency compared to humans. Automated ML is a real good approach here if you are working on Dynamics 365/Power Platform Data without knowing what algorithm to choose: it's often a good place to start.

When to Use Automated ML

When you want to train and tune your model using Azure Machine Learning for the specific target metric, you use automated ML. Automated ML empowers its users to identify an end-to-end machine learning pipeline despite their level of data science expertise.

Data scientists, analysts, and developers across enterprises use automated ML because:

- It doesn't require comprehensive programming knowledge to implement machine learning solutions.
- It saves time and resources.
- It leverages data science best practices.
- It follows agile problem-solving methods.

How Does the Automated ML Machine Learning Process Work?

Automated ML analyzes and simplifies each step of the machine learning process, from cleaning and handling a raw dataset to deploying a functional machine learning model. Conventional machine learning models are developed manually, and every step of the process is managed separately.

The steps in the machine learning process that are automated by Automated ML in the sequence they occur in the process are:

1. **Raw data processing.** This includes remodeling unstructured, raw data to a structured format and improving data quality by using methods like data cleaning, data integration, data transformation, and data reduction.

2. **Feature engineering and feature selection.** Automated ML uses domain knowledge of data and automates the process of creating features that are more compatible with machine learning algorithms by analyzing the input data and using data scaling and normalization techniques.

3. **Model selection.** Automated ML tests many different algorithms at once to select the one that works best for the business case. It is a possibility that data scientists might not have considered the same algorithm before.

4. **Hyperparameter optimization and parameter optimization.** Automated ML can fine-tune data, features, parameters, and hyperparameters of algorithms to generate accurate models relying on the trial-and-error method and established machine learning knowledge.

5. **Deployment with consideration for business and technology constraints.** Automated ML either deploys the best model, based on the metric criteria you defined, or deploys a specific model iteration from the ongoing experiment.

6. **Evaluation metric selection.** Automated ML provides an aggregate set of evaluation metrics that indicate how well the evaluation metrics for each category label performs, thus indicating how well the model performs for that label.

7. **Monitoring and problem checking.** Automated ML critically monitors the results to uncover insights and deal with the problems.

Moreover, Automated ML can be used for classification, regression, and forecasting.

Classification

Classification is a standard machine learning task in which models learn by using training data and implementing them to new data. It is a task that requires the use of machine learning algorithms to predict and assign the category to new data, based on learnings from its training data.

Azure Machine Learning offers featurization (when data-scaling and normalization techniques are used to create features that help ML algorithms to learn better), especially for classification tasks. You can create Automated ML experiments using Azure Machine Learning Studio by using the following steps:

1. Create a workspace (as mentioned in the previous section of this chapter). As a reminder again, you can sign up for a Free Azure Account and try Automated ML.
2. Sign into Azure Machine Learning Studio and select your subscription and workspace you created just now.
3. Now click the option Get started.
4. Go to the left pane under the Author section and select the option Automated ML.
5. If it is your first Automated ML experiment, you'll see an empty list and links to documentation.
6. Click on +New automated ML run.

Now, you must create and load your dataset (Figure 4.1). First, you need to upload your data file to your workspace. The reason behind uploading your data in the form of an Azure Machine Learning dataset in your workspace is because it assures you that your data is appropriately formatted for your experiment (Figure 4.2). Following are the steps to create and load the dataset. Of course, in a real production environment, you should connect to your own datastore like

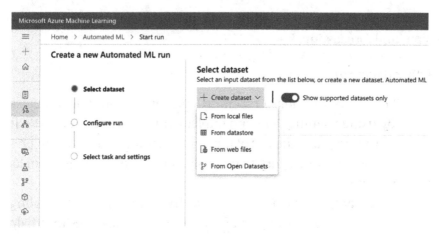

FIGURE 4.1 Select dataset.

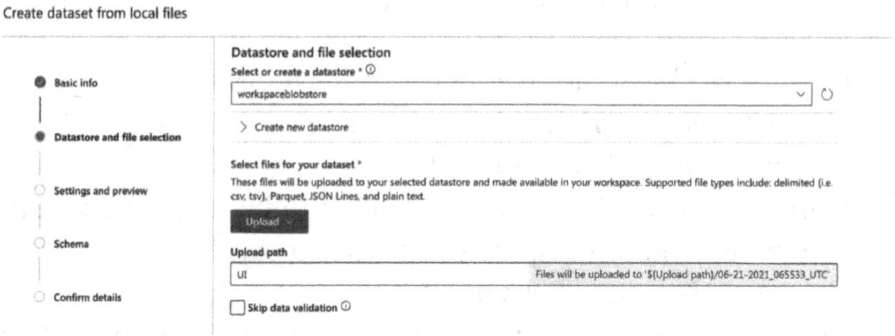

FIGURE 4.2 Upload your data file.

your Azure Data Lake Storage or even your Synapse Analytics. You can also try to use Azure Open Data sets, which will give you some basic examples to try with real datasets very fast.

To create a new dataset, select the +Create dataset drop-down and choose option From local files to upload your dataset.

1. When a Basic info form is opened, name your dataset and provide an optional description. Make sure that the default setting of your dataset type is Tabular because the automated ML interface currently only supports TabularDatasets.

2. Click on the Next button on the bottom left.
3. It takes you to Datastore and the file selection form; select the default datastore Workspaceblobstore (Azure Blob Storage). Upload your data file here to make it available to your workspace.
4. Click Browse.
5. Choose the file from your local computer that you downloaded as a prerequisite.
6. Give a unique name to your dataset and give an optional description if needed.
7. Select Next on the bottom left and upload it to the default container by selecting the Next button on the bottom left.
8. You will see the Settings and preview form based on the file type after the uploading is completed.
9. Verify that the Settings and preview form is populated as follows and select Next.
   a. File format – Delimited
   b. Delimiter – Comma
   c. Encoding – UTF-8
   d. Column headers – All files have the same headers.
   e. Skip rows – None
10. The Schema form allows for further configuration of your data for the current experiment if you don't want to make any selections. Select Next.
11. Verify the information on the Confirm details form such as the Basic info, Datastore and file selection and Settings and preview forms.
12. If everything is as expected, Select Create to complete the creation of your dataset.
13. Now select your dataset from the list.
14. Review the Data preview, then select Close.
15. Select Next.

Now you have to configure the run (Figure 4.3).

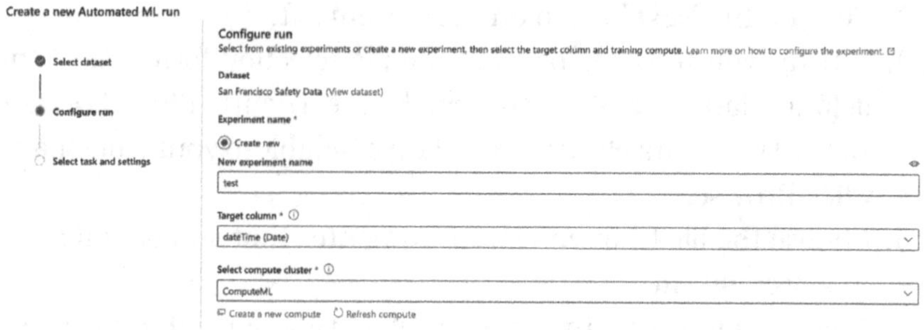

FIGURE 4.3 Configure run.

All you have to do is set up your experiment. This setup involves experiment design tasks such as specifying the column you want the prediction from and selecting the size of your computing environment.

1. Select the Create a new radio button.
2. You will see the Configure Run form as follows:
   a. Enter this experiment name: enter any unique name of your choice; here we are using my-1st-Automated ML-experiment.
   b. Select y as the target column, which you want to predict.
   c. Click on the option +Create a new compute and configure the compute target. We select compute target here because it is a local or cloud-based resource environment that runs your training script or hosts your service deployment. For now, we are using cloud-based compute. Then you will have a virtual machine form to set up your compute:
      i. Virtual machine – Dedicated
      ii. Virtual machine type – CPU (central processing unit)
      iii. Virtual machine size – Standard_DS12_V2
   d. Select Next and see the Configure settings form:
      i. Compute name – Automated ML-compute
      ii. Min/Max nodes – Min nodes: 1, Max nodes: 6
      iii. Idle seconds before scale down – 120 (default)
      iv. Advanced settings – None

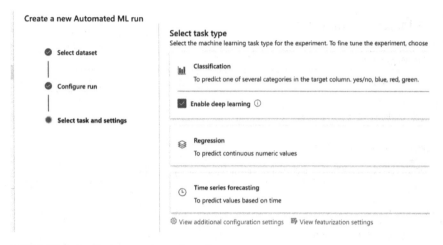

FIGURE 4.4 Select task and settings.

e. Click on Create button to create a compute target.

f. Creation could take a couple of minutes, but once it's created, select your new compute target from the drop-down list.

g. Click on the Next button.

3. To complete the setup for your automated ML experiment, Go to Task type and settings form and specify the machine learning task type and configuration settings (Figure 4.4).

a. It will ask you the machine learning task type. Select Classification.

b. Go to View additional configuration settings (Figure 4.5) and fill the fields as follows.

   i. Primary metric – AUC-weighted

   ii. Explain the best model – Enable

   iii. Blocked algorithms – None

   iv. Exit criterion – Training job time (hours): 24; Metric score threshold: None

   v. Validation – Validation type: Train-validation split; Number of validations: 10%

   vi. Concurrency – Max concurrent iterations: 5

   vii. Now click on Save Button.

Additional configurations   ✕

Primary metric ⓘ

| AUC weighted | ⌄ |

☑ **Explain best model** ⓘ

Blocked algorithms ⓘ

| A list of algorithms that Automated ML will not use during training. |

⌄ Exit criterion

Training job time (hours) ⓘ

| 24 |

When enabling deep learning, Automated ML recommends a max experiment time of 24 hours (note: Automated ML will automatically end the run early when best score is reached).

Metric score threshold ⓘ

| Metric score threshold |

⌄ Validation

Validation type ⓘ

| Train-validation split | ⌄ |

Percentage validation of data * ⓘ

| 10 |

Automated ML recommends that between 10 and 30 percent of data is held out for validation

⌄ Concurrency

Max concurrent iterations ⓘ

| 5 |

FIGURE 4.5 Additional configurations.

4. Click on Finish to run the experiment. The Run Detail screen pops up in front of you with the Run status at the top as the experiment begins. This status renews with the progress of the experiment. Notifications populate the top right corner of the studio to notify the status of your experiment.

Now we will explore the models:

1. Go to the Models tab to observe the algorithms (models) that have been tested. By default, the models are sequenced according to their metric score as they complete.
2. Select the Algorithm name of whichever model is completed to examine its performance details, while you wait for other experiment models to complete.

Moving on to the deployment of the model, deployment is the integration of the model. It is done to predict potential areas of opportunities for new data. The automated machine learning interface empowers you to select and deploy the best model. The steps to deploy your model are:

1. Select the best model, based on the chosen metric.
2. Click the Deploy button in the top-left.
3. Populate the Deploy a model pane as follows:
   a. Deployment name – my-Automated ML-deploy
   b. Deployment description – my first automated machine learning experiment deployment
   c. Compute type – Select Azure Compute Instance (ACI)
   d. Enable authentication – Disable
   e. Use custom deployments – Disable
4. Select Deploy.
5. After you click the Deploy button, you will observe a green success message at the top of the Run screen, and a status message appears in the Model summary pane under Deploy status.
6. To check the deployment status periodically, select Refresh.

Regression

Regression is a common supervised learning task. Based on independent predictors, the regression models predict numerical output values. The main objective of regression is to estimate how one independent predictor variable impacts the others and how they relate to each other, for example, how an automobile price is based on gas mileage, safety rating, and so on.

Time-series Forecasting

Time-series forecasting is a process of using historical data to predict future observations. Most of the companies today are using time-series forecasting to develop and innovate their business strategies. They mainly use it for tasks like financial planning, resource planning, inventory planning, and capacity planning. It has become a fundamental part of any business, whether it is revenue, inventory, sales, or customer demand.

In general, when we create a machine learning model, we analyze different algorithms and hyperparameter values, but when we focus mainly on time-series forecasting, we also need to consider seasonality and the effects of holidays. So, it becomes tricky to build a model with all these complex considerations. So, instead of manually performing all the tasks, we can switch to Automated Machine Learning. Automated ML can automate tasks like algorithm selection, hyperparameter value search, and data featurization, including holidays. It can help you find the best machine learning model for your data.

An automated time-series experiment is administered as a multivariate regression problem. Former time-series values are "pivoted" and become additional dimensions for the regressor together with other predictors. Unlike classical time series methods, this approach has an advantage of consolidating multiple contextual variables and their relationship to one another during training.

Automated ML creates and ranks several models based on the accuracy of the results, which can be examined to decide which one is the best solution to your problem. Once you have found the perfect model, you can instantly add input and output stages, and deploy it as a service.

Making machines that learn from experience should eventually eliminate the programming effort of data scientists. Automated Machine Learning endeavors to empower data scientists and data analysts to figure out answers to the following questions intelligently:

- Which features should we select to train the models?
- How do we select algorithms?
- Which parameters should we select to tune?

Which Features Should We Select to Train the Models?

While exploring your data, you will discern that your data might need preprocessing. It is wise to check the data for common issues (also known as data guardrails) to identify potential issues within the data before being used as inputs to train the machine learning algorithm.

It is crucial to decide which features to use for training the models. Casting all features as inputs for training will not necessarily provide a good model. Hence, it is essential to select relevant features first.

To do so, we need to understand the concepts of feature engineering and featurization first.

Feature engineering is the method of creating features using domain knowledge of the input data to help machine learning (ML) algorithms learn better and provide better results.

In Azure Machine Learning, when techniques like data-scaling and normalization are collectively used with feature engineering to make the process easier, it is termed as "featurization" in Automated ML experiments.

By default, normalization and data scaling techniques are applied to your data in every automated machine learning experiment. To configure featurization techniques in Azure Machine Learning Studio, you should open View featurization settings. Then enable Automatic featurization in the Additional configuration settings form. This way, the default featurization techniques are applied.

Let's investigate the techniques that are automatically applied to your data after enabling automatic featurization:

- **Drop high cardinality or no variance features.** This feature drops high cardinality and low variance variables from training and validation sets. It is applied when your data consists of missing values, or the same value across all rows, or with high cardinality (e.g., identification numbers, email addresses, or usernames).

- **Impute missing values.** This feature is applied to replace missing data with substituted values, mostly when numeric values are missing from your data; it imputes those missing values with the average of values in the column. And for categorical values, it imputes with the most prevalently appearing value.

- **Generate more features.** This feature helps you create things like year, month, day, day of the week, day of year, quarter, week of the year, hour, minute, second, and so on. For text, it helps you to create unigrams, bigrams, and trigrams based on term frequency.

- **Transform and encode.** This feature transforms numeric values with few unique values into categorical values. One-hot encoding is used for low-cardinality categorical features; it represents categorical variables as binary vectors. One-hot-hash encoding is used for high-cardinality categorical features.

- **Word embeddings.** This feature converts vectors of text tokens into sentence vectors by using a pre-trained model. Each word embedding vector in a document is aggregated with the rest to produce a document feature vector.

■ **Cluster distance.** This feature trains a k-means clustering model on all numeric columns. It produces new features that include the distance between each sample and the centroid of each cluster.

Moving on to our next concept to help us improve our data is Data Guardrails.

Data guardrails are a means to identify potential issues like class imbalance or missing values with your data. They also assist you in taking remedial actions for enhanced results.

Data guardrails are applied for:

■ **SDK experiments.** You have selected the parameters "featurization": auto or validation=auto in your Automated MLConfig object.
■ **Studio experiments.** You have selected enabled status for automatic featurization.

Data guardrails display results in one of the three states:

1. **Passed.** When there are no issues found with your data, and you require no action.
2. **Done.** When Automated ML took some corrective measures to improve your data, and you need to review these changes to ensure that the changes align with the expected results.
3. **Alerted.** When an issue is detected that cannot be resolved. In this case, it is advised that you revise and fix the issue.

Data guardrails that are supported include those noted in Table 4.1.

TABLE 4.1 Data guardrails.

Guardrail	Status	Triggering Condition
Missing feature values imputation	Passed	Your training data is free of missing feature values.
	Done	Your training data contains missing feature values and was imputed.
High cardinality feature handling	Passed	No high-cardinality features were detected in your inputs.
	Done	Your inputs contained high-cardinality features and were handled.
Validation split handling	Done	If the training data contained *fewer than 20,000 rows* and the validation configuration setting was set to "auto."
		Each iteration of the trained model was validated using cross-validation.
		If the training data contained *more than 20,000 rows* and the validation configuration was set to "auto."
		For validation of the model, the input data has been split into a training dataset.
Class balancing detection	Passed	Your inputs were analyzed, and all classes are balanced in your training data.
	Alerted	Detected imbalanced classes in your inputs. Fix the balancing problem.
	Done	Detected imbalanced classes in your inputs and the sweeping logic have determined to apply balancing.
Memory issues detection	Passed	The horizon, lag, rolling window were analyzed, and no potential out-of-memory issues were detected.
	Done	The selected values (horizon, lag, rolling window) will potentially cause your experiment to run out of memory. The lag or rolling-window configurations have been turned off.
Frequency detection	Passed	All data points are aligned with the detected frequency when the time series was analyzed.
	Done	Data points that do not align with the detected frequency during the analysis of time series were detected. These data points were removed from the dataset.

These were the associated statuses that you might encounter while submitting your experiment. Before you begin developing and training the machine learning model, you need to perform some checks like data preprocessing and data guardrail.

How to Select Algorithms

After preparing your data for training, you should focus on choosing the right algorithms for your model. There are many algorithms devised for machine learning tasks:

- **Classification.** There are many classification algorithms, of which you need to choose which one works best for your dataset. Here are some commonly used classification algorithms: logistics regression, gradient boosting, LightGBM, k-nearest neighbors, decision trees, random forest, XGBoost, naïve Bayes, and many more.
- **Regression.** Some standard regression algorithms are elastic net, LightGBM, gradient boosting, decision trees, k-nearest neighbors, LARS lasso, random forest, linear regression, and many more.
- **Time-series forecasting.** Some of the commonly used time-series forecasting algorithms include auto-ARIMA, linear regression, LightGBM, dilated CNN, mean forecast, ARIMA, ETS, and many more.

Choosing the right algorithm depends on the business problem and the machine learning task. Data scientists try many of these algorithms depending upon the task, the dataset size, their experience, or the ones that can easily be interpreted and explained. Sometimes, their main concern is the speed of the algorithms. For example, it is more likely for them to choose a less persuasive algorithm that can quickly provide results. This gives them an idea of which algorithms they should try next.

Which Parameters Should We Select to Tune?

There are three categories of data that are handled by your application during model training:

1. Input data, or training data, is a collection of individual instances that are important to solve your machine learning problem. This data is responsible for accurately making predictions during the training process to configure the model about new instances of similar data. However, these values can never be a part of your model.
2. Model parameters are the variables that are used to adjust to your data by the machine learning technique chosen by you. For example, a deep neural network (DNN) is considered as a model parameter. It is composed of neurons which are also called processing nodes; operations are performed in each data as it travels through the network. Each node has a weight value after your DNN is trained. This shows how much impact it has on the final prediction. These weights are examples of your model's parameters.
3. Hyperparameters are the variables whose values must be defined outside the training process. They oversee the training process itself. For example, to set up a deep neural network, you have to first decide the number of hidden layers you want to use between the input layer and the output layer and the number of nodes used by each layer. Hyperparameters are configuration variables that are not directly related to the training data. Unlike other parameters, which change during a training job, hyperparameters remain ordinarily constant during a job.

The process of choosing the right hyperparameters is known as hyperparameter optimization. Selecting the right hyperparameters is a crucial step because they directly control the training algorithm's behavior and have a massive impact on the model's performance, which is being trained. For example, if the learning speed is too low, the model will blow the data's essential patterns. However, if the speed is high, it may suffer collisions.

Every hyperparameter chosen by you has the potential to increase the number of trials needed for a thriving tuning job. Three standard algorithms help in the selection of hyperparameters:

1. **Grid search** uses learning rate, and number layers to train the algorithm for all combinations, and after that, it analyzes the performance using the "cross-validation" technique. This technique validates that your trained model captured most of the patterns from the dataset. Another technique best used to perform validation is "K-fold cross validation," which provides adequate data for training and validations. Grid search is a prevalent technique for the implementation of hyperparameters. Grid search needs to build two sets of hyperparameters:
   a. Learning rate
   b. Number of layers
2. **Random search** uses random combinations of the hyperparameters to find the most appropriate solution for your model. It examines random combinations from a range of values and evaluates sets from a specified probability distribution to optimize with random search. For example, instead of checking all the innumerable samples, we can check 1,000 random parameters. The only drawback of using this technique is it does not use historical information from previous experiments to choose the next set. Also, it is challenging to predict the next set of experiments.
3. **Bayesian optimization,** unlike random or grid, keeps track of past evaluation results so that new samples improve the primary metric. These evaluation results are also used to create a probabilistic model by mapping hyperparameters:

   P (score | hyperparameters)

   This technique can be used if you have enough budget to explore the hyperparameter space.

Ensemble Models

Automated Machine Learning by default supports ensemble models. To understand what ensemble models do in automated machine learning, let's first understand what it is.

The ensemble is a learning technique that consolidates multiple base models to produce one improved and optimal predictive model. Ensemble methods are like meta-algorithms that decrease variance and bias and, as a result, improve predictions. Automated machine learning uses two methods to combine models:

1. **Voting.** This method predicts results based on the weighted average of predicted class probabilities for classification tasks and predicted regression targets for regression tasks.
2. **Stacking.** This method combines heterogeneous models to train a meta-model based on the individual model's output. The default meta-models are LogisticRegression for classification tasks and ElasticNet for regression/forecasting tasks.

Automated Machine Learning uses the Caruana ensemble selection algorithm with sorted ensemble initialization to decide which models to use. This algorithm starts the ensemble with five models with the best scores and confirms if the models are within a 5 percent threshold of the best score to avoid a low initial ensemble. Then a new model is added to the existing ensemble for each ensemble iteration, and the score is calculated. If a new model has improved the existing ensemble score, it is updated, and the new model is added.

Designer Authoring Experience in Azure ML Studio

Azure Machine Learning Designer is a visual canvas that connects datasets and modules on an interactive environment to build, test, and deploy machine learning predictive models by using a drag and drop interface without any prior knowledge of coding. However, it provides an option to bring in custom R or Python if needed. It is considered as a successor of ML Studio (Classic).

Azure ML Designer enables you to build custom machine learning models, and it helps you to make a machine learning API quickly. It provides a set of prebuilt modules, customizable Python, or R scripts that are connected to make a ready-for-use machine learning API in your code. Businesses are increasingly adopting machine learning to create solutions for different types of business problems, and Azure Machine Learning Designer can bring a much wider audience. They only need data to build both analytical and predictive models, with minimal or no data science expertise.

Let's investigate prerequisites of building machine learning models with the Designer core authoring experience:

- It is essential to configure an Azure Machine Learning work-space first. So, create an Azure account on the Azure Machine Learning site.
- Take a subscription and create a workspace for your models.
- While setting up the wizard, you need to choose a public or private endpoint of your resulting model. Then it would help if you choose whether or not you are working with sensitive data before choosing how keys are handled.
- In Azure, sensitive data is processed in a "high business impact workspace," which decreases the diagnostic data and adds extra levels of encryption.
- The workspace consists of several tools that help in the development and management of machine learning models, including designing, training, computations, and storage. It also helps you to increase the value of your training data set and label existing data.
- To create an ML model, you can choose from three main options:
  1. Work with the Azure ML Python SDK in a Jupyter-style notebook.
  2. Use automated training tools.
  3. The low-code drag-and-drop Designer surface.
- Since we are learning to work with Designer first, we will be continuing with it. The Designer uses shared resources

available and uses them to create models. Shared resources used by Designer include:

- Pipelines
- Datasets
- Compute resources
- Registered models
- Published pipelines
- Real-time endpoints

We have covered some of these resources in previous sections of this chapter. Let's understand the rest, one by one, to see how these resources help in building ML models.

Azure Machine Learning Pipelines

Azure Machine Learning pipeline is an autonomously executable workflow of a whole machine learning task (Figure 4.6). Subtasks in the pipeline are encapsulated as a series of steps. These pipelines can do just about anything from making a call for Python script to more complex tasks. Your pipelines should majorly concentrate on machine learning tasks such as:

- Importing, cleaning, validating data and transformation, normalization, and staging as done in the data preparation process.
- Training configuration including logging/reporting configurations and parameterizing arguments and file paths.
- Training and verifying the results efficiently and repeatedly. High-level performance can be achieved by specifying specific data subsets, distributed processing, different hardware compute resources, and progress monitoring.
- Deployment tasks, which include versioning, provisioning, scaling, and access control.

To create pipelines, Designer enables you to drag and drop steps onto your design surface. The inputs and outputs of every step are displayed visibly. The drag and drop feature to create data connections

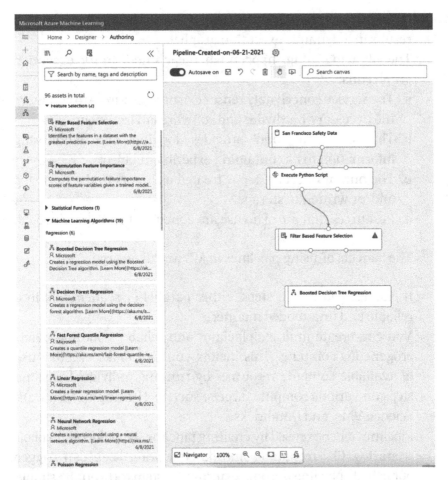

FIGURE 4.6 Pipeline.

empowers you to understand and alter the dataflow of your pipeline instantly. The following are the high-level steps that occur when you run the pipeline object:

1. Calculate the requirements for each step:
   a. Hardware compute resources
   b. OS resources (like Docker image(s))
   c. Software resources (like Conda/virtual env dependencies)
   d. Data inputs

2. It determines the dependencies between various steps, which results in a dynamic execution graph.
3. The following things happen when each node in the execution graph runs:
   a. The service conceivably reuses existing resources to configure the necessary hardware and software environment.
   b. The step runs and provides logging and monitoring information to its containing experiment object.
   c. The output of every step is treated as inputs to the next step and/or written to storage.
   d. Resources that are of no use are concluded and disconnected.

The benefits of using pipelines in ML workflow are:

■ It enables you to run steps, either parallel or sequentially in a reliable and unattended manner.
■ You can create multiple pipelines and reliably coordinate heterogeneous compute. This means you can make effective use of available compute resources by running individual pipeline steps on various compute targets, such as HDInsight, GPU Data Science VMs, and Databricks.
■ Pipelines can be reused by creating pipeline templates for explicit scenarios, like retraining and batch-scoring. You can trigger published pipelines from external systems through simple REST calls.
■ For tracking and versioning your data sources, inputs, and outputs, you can use pipelines SDK.
■ Pipelines enable data scientists to collude across all areas of the machine learning design process.

Azure ML pipeline is a compelling resource that begins with providing value in the early developing stages. Its value rises as the team and projects progress. Azure Machine Learning pipelines are designed to help you build, optimize, and manage machine learning workflows.

Registered Model

Models are identified by names and their versions in the workspace. Once you have a model, you register it on your workspace. It helps you to maintain a record of all the models in your Azure Machine Learning workspace. A registered model is like a logical container that contains one or more files that collectively contribute to your model. After the registration process is completed, you can then download or deploy the registered model and receive all the registered files. A registered model that is in use by an active deployment cannot be deleted.

Published Pipelines

Once you have it up and running, you can publish your pipeline to run with different inputs. After publishing your pipeline, you can configure a REST endpoint, enabling you to rerun the pipeline from any platform or stack. A pipeline endpoint empowers you to submit new pipeline runs from external applications using REST calls. However, you cannot send or receive data in real-time using a pipeline endpoint.

Published pipelines are used to train or retrain models, process new data, perform batch inferencing, and much more. It runs on the compute resources assigned by you in the pipeline draft for each module. The designer can create the same published pipeline object as the SDK.

You can publish multiple pipelines to a single pipeline endpoint by designating which pipeline version to run.

Real-Time Endpoints

When you want prediction results for the application in real time, this is where real-time endpoint comes in. The real-time endpoint works as a bridge between an external application and your scoring model through an interface. You just have to call a real-time endpoint to return prediction results to the application in real time.

To have a prediction in real time, you need to perform real-time inferencing by deploying a pipeline as the real-time endpoint. Then, to make a call to this real-time endpoint, you need to pass the API key that was created when you deployed the endpoint. You should deploy real-time endpoints to an Azure Kubernetes Service cluster.

Now that we have learned about the shared resources used by Designer, we can move on to the step-by-step process of building a model by using Designer.

Start by signing in to Azure Machine Learning Studio. Now follow these steps:

Step 1: Source the data into Azure Machine Learning Studio.
There are two ways to source the data in Azure. You can either import your data from multiple sources or use the already available sample data in ML Studio. The data you import will be considered as the "raw" data. The steps to do so are:

1. Click +NEW button at the bottom of the ML Studio to create a new experiment.
2. Then select Experiment accompanied by Blank Experiment.
3. To upload the data, search for a data set in the search box in the top-left side of the screen.
4. Now, drag and drop your dataset on the experiment canvas.

You have successfully imported the data for your model in this stage. Now you have to process it to use it analytically.

Step 2: Data pre-processing. This is a critical step that is performed before using the dataset for predictions. This process accounts for the missing and incorrect values from the dataset. Let's prepare the data needed for our model. Here we will follow the steps required to delete a column that has missing values.

1. Find a search box on the top-left corner, enter Select Columns. Click the Select Columns in Dataset. This module allows you to include or exclude the columns.

2. Now, drag and connect the input port of Select Columns in Dataset module with the output port of let's say XYZdata module.
3. Click the Select Columns in Dataset module.
4. In the Properties pane, choose and click the Launch Column Selector.
5. On the left, click the With rules option.
6. Choose the All Columns option under the Begin with option.
7. Choose the Exclude option and Column names from the two dropdown lists you see. Then choose the Normalized losses option from the list of columns displayed on the screen.
8. To close the column selector window, click the tick mark button on the bottom right of the window.
9. At this point, except Normalized-losses, all the columns will pass through.
10. Just when you have connected the first two modules, drag the clean missing data module and combine it with the Select Columns in Dataset module in the experiment window.
11. Remove the rows with the missing values, select Remove entire row option under the Cleaning mode options in the Properties pane.
12. Double-click on the module named Clean missing data and type the comment "Remove missing value rows."
13. Click the RUN button placed at the bottom of the page.

Now, you have successfully preprocessed the raw data.

Step 3: Defining features for your ML model. A feature is an individual quantifiable or measurable property of interest. The set of features in a dataset are often in their raw state and do not sustain enough optimal information to train a model. In some cases, it helps to remove objectionable or incompatible features, and this is known as **feature selection**. In other cases, it helps if we transform some features into a different representation to improve model performance by providing better information to the model. This process is called **feature engineering.** To select appropriate features, it is important to have the knowledge of the problem you expect your model to solve. Following are the steps of how you can define features for your ML model:

- Search and drag another Select column in the Dataset module.
- Connect the input port of this Select Column with the left output port of the Clean Missing Data module.
- Double-click the module and type "Select features for prediction."
- Go to the Properties pane and Choose Launch Column selector.
- Select With Rules option.
- Select No Columns option, under the Begin With option.
- From the two dropdown lists, select Include and Column Names, accordingly.
- Elect the column names (features) that you need for your model. The selected features will then appear in the text box given.
- Confirm the selection of features by clicking on the Tick mark button.

You have successfully defined features of your predictive model.

Step 4: Choosing the right algorithm. There are two ways to choose the right algorithm: you can use a cheat sheet provided by Microsoft or use the following steps:

1. You can choose the regression algorithm if you want to predict a value. To forecast the future using a regression algorithm, all you need to do is estimate the relationship between variables. It can be used for product demand estimation, equipment servicing priorities determination, sales figures prediction, and so on. There are eight types of regression algorithms:

   a. Ordinal regression
   b. Poisson regression
   c. Fast Forest Quantile regression
   d. Linear regression
   e. Bayesian regression
   f. Neural network regression

g. Decision Forest regression

h. Boosted decision tree regression

2. If you want to determine and predict rare data points, you can choose from the following algorithms:

   ▪ One class SVM.

   ▪ PCA-based anomaly detection, which can be used for abnormal equipment readings, fraud exposure, and so on.

3. If you want to incorporate similar data into one set, you should use the K-means clustering algorithm. It can be used for customer segmentation, customer taste prediction, and so on.

4. If you want your prediction to lie between two categories (e.g., if you want to know if the tweet is positive or negative, and the algorithm should predict either "yes" or "no"), the following algorithms can be used:

   ▪ Two-class SVM

   ▪ Two-class averaged perception

   ▪ Two-class Bayes point machine

   ▪ Two-class decision forest

   ▪ Two-class logistic regression

   ▪ Two-class boosted decision tree

   ▪ Two-class decision jungle

   ▪ Two-class locally deep SVM

   ▪ Two-class neural network

5. If you want to predict the nature of your data between multiple categories (e.g., predicting the mood of a tweet), the options are:

   ▪ Multiclass logistic regression

   ▪ Multiclass neural network

   ▪ Multiclass decision forest

   ▪ Multiclass decision jungle

   ▪ One-vs.-all multiclass

Based on your business needs, you can choose the algorithm. Now we move on to the training and deploying of models using Designer.

How do you train and deploy models using Designer?

- You need to find a Train Model module under the Machine Learning category and then Expand Train, to drag the Train Model module into the pipeline.
- Attach the training dataset into the right input of the Train Model and put untrained mode on the left. Make sure that your training dataset contains labeled columns. Otherwise, it would get ignored.
- To label columns, go to the Edit column in the right panel of the module and choose a column containing outcomes the model can use for training.
  - For classification problems, the label column must have either categorical values or discrete values.
  - For regression problems, the label column must have numeric data to represent the response variable.
  - Azure Machine Learning will attempt to gather the appropriate label column using the dataset's metadata. Suppose you fail to specify which label column to use. If it indents the wrong column, use the column selector to correct it.
- Submit the pipeline once you are done.

This is how you build a machine learning model using Designer.

Notebooks

There is no doubt in admitting that Azure ML Studio is a persuasive tool for a data scientist, as it provides the flexibility to experiment with out-of-the-box datasets and machine learning models rapidly. But Jupyter notebook is also a de facto tool for working on data science tasks.

However, deployment of Jupyter Notebook as a web service is entirely a different story. Azure ML Studio provides an option to create and host your Jupyter notebooks online and deploy it as a web service while creating models through it.

Let's get started with Azure Jupyter Notebook.

Step 1:
1. Go to https://studio.azureml.net/ and login to your workspace.
2. On the left panel, there is a Notebooks tab; click on it.
3. Then at the bottom, you will see New; click it.

Step 2: Now create a Python file for our ML experiment.
1. Click on the File icon.
2. Enter your file name >> File type: Python Notebook >> Target directory: your directory.
3. Click Create to make a Python notebook.

Step 3: Now you need to create an Azure Machine Learning virtual machine. Click on +New VM to create one.
- Enter your VM name.
- For VM type: If you are a beginner, choose your system type as STANDARD_DS1_V2.
- Once you are done creating a Notebook VM, see that it goes to the Compute section under Manage panel.

Step 4: Run the Notebook. You need to verify if our Notebook is working accurately or not.
- Validate your Notebook Virtual Machine if it is on the running level.
- Move the cursor to the middle of your Notebook and observe the Create text cell with a Dialog; click it.
- The cell is an empty markdown cell by default, so choose Convert code cell for changing.

When you are done with this, you are ready for the coding part. Let's write a Python "Hello World" program to ensure that the Notebook is working. There is a run button at the top right side of the Notebook and in each cell also.

Step 5: Uploading the dataset.

1. There is a vertical arrow on your Notebook's left side, which is an icon for uploading datasets.
2. Use any dataset available in your local system.
3. There is an Upload files icon; click on it >> then Navigate your dataset folder and choose file >> Open >> select target directory>> Upload.

Now you can see the dataset visually in your directory.

 ## AZURE MACHINE LEARNING SERVICE

The Azure ML service is an open platform to create ML solutions using Python. It provides tools to scale and automate training, deployment, and monitoring of ML models easily and seamlessly.

Before the introduction of Azure Machine learning service, in order to use machine learning in a production environment, you were required to bring together a bunch of data services to support the full machine learning lifecycle, for example, the following data services:

- **Azure blob storage or Azure data lake storage** are storage solutions for data. It is important to bring these solutions together because models cannot be trained without data.
- **Virtual machines, Azure HDInsight, and Azure Databricks** are brought together to run the code.
- **Virtual network** functions as a security boundary, securing your data by isolating your Azure resources from the public internet. You can bring your virtual network to figure out your computing and data in the same virtual network, or you can also use Azure virtual network to your on-premises network to securely train your models and access your deployed models for reasoning.

▪ **Azure key vault** is a cloud-hosted service to manage and secure your credentials, authorize access for certificates, and many other secrets. You have full control of the keys to access and encrypt your data. Administrators have the power to grant or revoke access to the keys.

▪ **Docker containers** image is a stand-alone, executable package of software used to run your experiment repeatedly because it has everything needed to run an application such as a consistent set of ML libraries, code, system tools, and settings. It uses the Azure Container registry, which is a private Docker registry service to store those Docker containers and then put them inside your virtual network.

▪ **Azure Kubernetes Service** is an orchestration service used to deploy, scale, and manage Docker containers and container-based applications across a cluster of container hosts, including them as well in virtual network.

Bringing all this together in the same virtual network to get machine learning models to work together consumes a lot of time. But Microsoft eliminated this complexity with Azure Machine learning service.

Azure ML Services is a managed infrastructure for experienced data scientists and AI developers who are proficient in Python. It is a service used to build and deploy models, using any tool or framework.

The benefits of using Azure Machine learning service are:

▪ It provides end-to-end ML lifecycle management.
▪ It keeps track of all of your experiments.

- It has built-in capabilities like version control and model repro-ducibility to replicate any experiment by storing everything related to your experiment such as code, config, environment details, parameter settings, and so on.
- It facilitates you to encapsulate your model in a container so that you can deploy it to Azure on-premises or on IoT devices. The container in which you encapsulate your model can be easily managed and scaled.
- It has Notebook VM, which is a cloud-based workstation integrated into Azure Machine Learning service and specifically created for data scientists to make it easy for them to start locally and then easily compute it in Azure. It helps developers and data scientists to perform operations supported by Azure Machine Learning Python SDK using Jupyter notebook.
- It uses popular frameworks like TensorFlow and scikit-learn and offers a powerful toolset to operate ML experiments. It enables you to deploy models into production in a third-party service like Docker.

CHAPTER FIVE

Deep Dive in Machine Learning Custom Models

N THE PREVIOUS CHAPTER, we discussed how Microsoft enables you to leverage the power of AI and ML in your projects, even when you are not an expert in the data science field.

In this chapter, we will learn about the two tools of the Azure AI platform – Azure CLI Extension and Visual Studio Code – and how you can use these tools for your benefit.

AZURE CLI EXTENSION

Azure Command Line Interface (CLI) is a set of commands that provides cross-platform command-line experience and is also used to create and manage resources. It is designed to get you working quickly with Azure, as it is available across Azure services.

Azure CLI is used to automate day-to-day repetitive operations. It enables you to schedule these tasks and also deploy them. Especially if you are deploying hundreds of resources, it is the perfect way to automate the process. Some key features of CLI that make it convenient to use are:

■ **Interactive mode.** This mode guides you through available commands, places you in an interactive shell with command descriptions, examples, and auto-completion, and leads you on whether you need parameters. To use Azure CLI interactive mode, just type the following command: az interactive.

■ **Multiple output formats.** As a default output format, Azure CLI uses JSON, but it also offers output in other formats. The following are the output formats with argument values:

  ■ **JSON.** JSON string. This setting is the default.
  ■ **JSONC.** Colorized JSON.
  ■ **YAML.** A machine-readable alternative to JSON.
  ■ **Table.** ASCII table with keys as column headings.
  ■ **TSV.** Tab-separated values with no keys.
  ■ **None.** No output other than errors and warnings.

■ **Querying with JMESPath.** JSON has a query language called JMESPath that enables you to select and modify data from CLI output. All commands in the Azure CLI supports query argument to execute a JMESPath query.

■ **Cross-platform.** Azure CLI is written in Python language, which means it is cross-platform and works on Windows, macOS, and Linux.

Some common commands that are used in CLI include:

■ az – CLI starting point.
  ■ az login – login to your Azure account
  ■ az account – manage the account
  ■ az groups – manage resource groups
  ■ az VM – virtual machines
  ■ az storage account – storage accounts
  ■ az Keyvault – key vault

- az webapp – web applications
- az sql server – SQL databases
- az cosmosdb – CosmosDB
- Globally available commands.
  - **Help.** This command displays reference information about the commands you display it with. It also displays related arguments and lists available subgroups and commands. For example, az group -h or az group -help will display all the groups, subgroups, and commands that might help you to write next command and get what you need.
  - **Output.** This command helps you to change the default output format that is JSON. As discussed, you can change the output to multiple formats mentioned previously.
  - **Query.** It is used to execute JMESPath query.
  - **Verbose.** This command returns the information about the resources created during an operation and other details related to it.
  - **Debug.** This command returns the information associated with CLI operations used for debugging purposes.

These are the commands in Azure CLI that are globally used. But in some cases, even the Azure CLI commands are not enough. For these cases, Azure CLI extensions are used. Azure CLI extensions are the enhancements to the CLI built to provide you with additional functionality. The extensions are Python wheels, which are a built-in Python code package that enables installation and uninstallation of small code packages on client applications easily. It can be run as CLI commands.

Now let us talk about Azure Cloud Shell, which is a command-line interface in the cloud. It helps you to explore which Azure CLI extensions are available by typing the following command:

```
az extension list-available --output table
```

This command will display a list; all you need to do now is choose any of these extensions to add functionality to the CLI. Using Azure CLI extensions is very simple. First, you need to install an extension to use it. To install a Find extension, type the following command:

```
az extension add --name Find (name of the
extension you want to install)
```

In this command, Find is the name of the extension we are installing. The Find extension is an AI-powered extension that enables you to discover CLI examples for a given context. Once you have successfully installed the extension, make sure you have the latest version of it; otherwise, you need to update the extension. And to do so, you can use the following command:

```
az extension update --name Find
```

This command will upgrade the Find extension to the latest version. If you want to know what any extension can do, then type the following command:

```
az find -h
```

The above command will display all the things the Find command can do. Now let us talk about how you can uninstall any extension when you are done with it. For uninstalling the extension, you must use the following command:

```
az extension remove --name <extension-name>
```

In this command, in place of extension name, write the name of the extension that you no longer need.

Azure CLI extensions make Azure CLI more powerful and valuable. It obtains access to experimental and pre-release commands along with the capability to write custom CLI interfaces.

VISUAL STUDIO CODE

Unlike other editors, Visual Studio (VS) Code is a powerful source code editor that combines the source code editor with effectual developer tooling, like debugging or IntelliSense code completion. It offers a pleasant edit-build-debug cycle without any friction, enabling you to spend less time fiddling with the environment and focus more time on executing your ideas.

VS Code extends all the abilities of a traditional text editor and initiates new productivity paths for developers. It has a rich ecosystem that supports JavaScript, TypeScript, and Node.js, and other languages like C++, C#, Java, Python, PHP, Go and runtimes (such as .NET and Unity).

Features that make the VS Code better from other text editors include:

- **Keyboard mappings.** VS Code offers Keymaps extensions that enable you to map all its shortcuts with other popular editors such as Sublime, Atom, Emacs, and even Eclipse. Due to this, you do not have to make much effort in switching from other editors to VS Code. To install a Keymap extension, you need to open the extensions search bar by pressing Ctrl/Cmd + K → Ctrl/Cmd + X. Then search for keymap.
- **Settings sync.** This extension enables you to share your configuration with other team members by exporting all of your VS Code settings into a Gist and sending them the ID to your Gist. Your team members can then synchronize all of your settings to their VS Code install and have them immediately applied.
- **Live share.** This enables you to pair up with your fellow developers. Your fellow developers can load up the project in their editor, and it also works for debugging. When you start a debug session, all team members get the same debug experience on

their editors. If someone changes the code, it will be changed in the editors of all other members.

- **Docker extension.** This extension enables you to perform all Docker actions in VS Code virtually. Based on the runtime you pick, VS Code automatically creates the requisite Docker files for your current project.
- **Azure app service.** This extension enables you to create new sites and deploy your code with a right-click. You can also use a pre-built shell script that automates checking your code into the right Gist endpoint to continuous setup delivery.

To get started with VS Code, the first thing you need to do is download the VS Code by going to https://code.visualstudio.com/. It is available for MAC, Linux, or Windows.

After downloading is complete, open VS Code; you will see a welcome screen. Here, you can create a new file or open a new folder. Let us create a new file.

VS Code supports hundreds of programming languages, extensions of which can be found in the VS Code marketplace. However, the default language support for a file is based on the filename extension. To add a new file extension to an existing language, go to files.associations setting, for example, if you want to add .myphp file extension to the PHP language:

```
"files.associations": {
"*.myphp": "php"
}
```

Let us now understand the interface pf VS Code:

- At the bottom, you will see a status bar; it contains helpful information such as current line number, programming language, and errors and warnings.
- On the left-hand side, you have an Activity bar; starting from the top, you will see:
  - File Explorer that contains your current files and folders.
  - Search, which can be used to search your files.

- Source control that helps you to track the changes you made in different versions of your files.
- Run view, which enables you to run and debug your code.
- Extension views where you can manage and download extensions for almost anything.
- In the center of the screen, you have the command palette. It is the control center for all the actions performed in the VS Code. Any action you perform in VS Code is mapped to command in the command palette.

To make VS Code a better editor for you, you need to install the correct extensions for the programming language you want to use. VS Code provides built-in support for some languages, but to have the best experience, install the extensions for the language you want to use.

You then need to go to keymaps to install keyboard shortcuts from other editors.

Another thing that can be customized here is your color theme. It enables you to choose any colors available in VS Code. Select the color theme option on the welcome screen to see the list of color themes. When you select a specific color, it shows the preview of the chosen color theme.

To learn about VS Code editing features, choose interactive playground. Here you will find examples of the code editor features such as multi-cursor editing. To see multiple cursors in action, you can click into the interactive panel.

There is literally nothing a VS Code cannot do. Any functionality that you need will either be supported by the editor or by someone who has created an extension for it.

Customer Churn Prediction

Customer churn, also known by the term customer attrition, is simply a tendency of customers to stop being a paying client to your business and abandon it. Businesses must take a proactive approach by recognizing the contributing factors responsible for customer attrition and enhancing customer retention by doing something about it. Customer attrition is not so good for businesses as it costs more to attract new loyal customers than preserving existing ones. Proactively predicting the customers who can leave your business is a critical insight that can help you minimize losses.

Azure Machine Learning can enable you to build models, even with relatively little or no experience in this area. To predict customer attrition, you can use historical customer data to train and develop churn prediction models in Azure Machine Learning. It will help if you have datasets that incorporate a true/false column for customer status. Models built based on these datasets can be used to identify which customer attributes are most prominent for retaining your customers.

To test different algorithms and choose the best one, you can use Automated Machine Learning (Automated ML). It automates the process for quicker deployment of a machine learning model with less manual work, while still producing the accurate results.

Customer Lifetime Value

Customer Lifetime Value is a metric that helps you to understand:

- How well are you resonating with your audience?
- How content are your customers with your products and services?
- What is it that you are doing right to fulfill their needs and what else can you do to make their experience impeccable?

Every business owner wants to know the answers to these questions. Sure, calculating customer lifetime value sounds tough and does not come under everyone's strong suit, but fortunately, learning how to calculate it is not that big of a deal. It does not require high-level arithmetic; in fact, you can calculate this metric repeatedly to establish map points as your business grows.

If you are successfully increasing the customer lifetime value, you are on the right track, and your customers love your product/services. Let us understand what customer lifetime value means.

Customer lifetime value (CLV), also referred to as lifetime value (LTV), is the average amount of expenditure your customers have made on your business over time. To calculate CLV, you need several data points:

- The average monthly transactions of your customer.
- The average amount spent per transaction by your customer.
- The average number of months your customers remain loyal.
- And then calculate the average gross margin.

Multiply all these numbers, and you will get the predictive CLV.

Product Recommendation System

Today, many e-commerce businesses are giving product recommendations to customers on their websites. It has become a standard feature for e-commerce websites. All businesses are adopting this feature rapidly because relevant product recommendations drive higher sales.

Microsoft has introduced a Microsoft Product recommendation system that does not cost anything more than the underlying Azure resources. You must train it first with some historical transaction data to get recommendations. It analyzes the data and discovers relationships between the products by comparing the interests of different users. For example, it looks for the products that have been purchased together by different users. Once your model is trained, you can add code to your website that requests recommendations by calling an application programming interface (API). You will be able to get two types of recommendations:

1. **Item-to-Item.** In this type of recommendation, you send an item number with the API, which then returns with the list of possible items that a customer might be looking for, for example on websites where they mention customers who bought Product A and also bought Product B.

2. **Personalized.** For this, you choose a particular user and send the recent transactions with the API, returning with product recommendations for that user.

The algorithm that is mostly used for such type of recommendations is the collaborative filtering approach. It combines the preferences of multiple users and comes up with a recommendation for a given user.

For item-to-item recommendation, the algorithm identifies the frequency of two items bought together by creating a matrix. Now the tricky part starts; the way it comes up with personalized recommendations requires matrix multiplication. Now let us investigate the architecture of the system:

■ The Product recommendation system deploys a web app. The same web app hosts the API that you call while training your model and which provides recommendations. It creates Azure Storage accounts for Blobs, Queues, and Tables and to perform training operations, it creates a Web Job Instance.

■ When you put in a request for training of your model, it gets the transaction data from blob storage and adds an entry for that model in the Model Registry Table. It also adds a message to the model queue.

■ When the Web Job Instance observes the new entry in the model queue, it trains the model. It puts the trained model in Blob storage and updates the entry in Model Registry to complete when it is finished.

■ When you send a request against recommendations, the process is much easier. It takes the model from Blob storage, loads it, runs the requests through it, and returns the recommendations. The only time-consuming task in this whole process is to get your transaction data into the format expected by a training job.

Before making the recommendations, the algorithm considers the interest of the user on products, which is why you need to define weights for every event type. For example, some default events are:

- If a user just clicked on a product – weight =1.
- If a user clicked on a recommendation link – weight = 2.
- If a user adds the product into the cart – weight = 3.
- If a user removes a product from the cart – weight = -1.
- If a user makes a purchase – weight = 4.

Indeed, if users make a purchase, they are more interested in the product than those who just clicked the product. That is why the weight of the purchase event is more than the weight of the clicking event.

This is how Microsoft's Product Recommendation System works.

6

Machine Learning with Dynamics 365 Use Cases

I N TODAY'S WORLD, WHEN every organization is searching for ways to enhance their productivity and work more efficiently, Microsoft has combined Dynamics 365 and machine learning to create solutions that can perform predictions and automate the processes to reduce the response time for your customers. The fusion of these two technologies can help you to build machine learning models by taking historical data and feeding it into analytical algorithms. Based on the predictions made by these models, organizations can identify their prime customers, and by leveraging their historical data and attributes, they can make informed decisions.

"You can have data without information, but you can't have information without data."

— *Daniel Keys Moran*

ML FOR FINANCE

Machine learning in finance extracts meaningful insights from unstructured data and provides precise results. The machine learning algorithms are implemented to learn from existing patterns in data, processes, and techniques useful to find different insights. The acquired information from the results is then used to solve complex problems crucial to the banking and finance divisions.

Today many financial organizations are taking advantage of machine learning for various reasons such as:

- Process automation using machine learning reduces costs.
- Machine learning provides better productivity and enhanced user experience, which results in increased revenue.
- Better acquiescence and reinforced security.

Let's investigate some machine learning use cases in the finance sector to better understand why it is used.

First Use Case: Process Automation

Machine learning solutions enable organizations to reduce manual work by automating repetitive processes for enhanced business productivity. Some automation uses cases that optimize costs, scale up services, and elevate customer experiences include:

- Chatbots
- Call-center automation
- Paperwork automation
- Gamification of employee training

A global financial services company, JPMorgan Chase, uses a machine learning technique called natural language processing to process legal documents and extract required information from them. If this process is performed manually, it will take up to around 360,000 labor hours to review 12,000 annual commercial credit agreements; whereas through machine learning, you can do it in just a few hours.

Second Use Case: Security

With the increase of users, transactions, and third-party integrations, security threats in finance are also increasing. In this case, machine learning algorithms are useful in fraud detection, as they analyze millions of data points that humans overlook. It also diminishes the number of false rejections and enhances the accuracy of real-time approvals.

Financial organizations can use this technology to monitor thousands of transaction parameters of every account in real time. Machine learning algorithms analyze every action of each user and evaluate if the attempted activity is the characteristic of that user. It helps recognize a client's frequent unusual behavior and helps companies spot fraudulent behavior with high precision and request additional user identification to authorize the transaction. Machine learning algorithms can assess a transaction in just a few seconds, so if there is even a 90 percent possibility that the user might be a fraud, the system can block the transaction altogether. Machine learning can also raise a flag when it detects many micropayments that could lead to money laundering techniques such as smurfing.

Companies like Paypal and Adyen invest heavily in machine learning security.

Third Use Case: Algorithmic Trading

Today more and more trading companies are switching to machine learning algorithms rather than human traders for more reliable trading decisions. Machine learning algorithms monitor real-time trading news. It can analyze thousands of data sources simultaneously to detect patterns and become a dominant force to enable stock price to go up or down.

Algorithmic trading empowers human traders with a slim advantage over the market average. And, considering the vast volumes of trading operations, even a small advantage can turn into significant profits.

These were some of the use cases that need machine learning solutions. One of the best machine learning solutions for finance is Dynamics 365 Finance application.

Fourth Use Case: Customer Data Management and Credit Scoring

It is crucial for banks and financial institutions to have efficient data management, which is central for business growth. All the massive data collected from transactions, social media, mobile communications, and so on can become a challenge for financial experts to process manually. Integrating machine learning techniques such as data analytics, data mining, and natural language processing can help you extract real intelligence from data.

Banks and financial companies have a lot of historical data. They use it to train machine learning models. These models can then be used for underwriting and credit-scoring tasks in real time.

Dynamics 365 Finance enhances and optimizes organizational operations by modernizing business and operational processes. Actionable insights powered by AI, machine learning, and predicted analytics enables management to make better business decisions for optimal operational planning. Key performance indicators (KPIs) can draw more effective customer management, budget planning, and expense management.

Dynamics 365 Finance empowers employees to automate functions such as task approvals, invoice automation, and vendor information approval workflows. This way, employees focus on other value-added tasks. Dynamics 365 Finance also possesses some enhanced capabilities like revenue recognition, proactive credit management, contract management, and more. Real-time KPIs and reporting allows quick operation oversight and cash flow visibility to drive operational decision making. All of this is connected by Dynamics 365 Finance to allow reporting from any device 24/7. General Data Protection Regulation (GDPR)–ready, Dynamics 365 Finance accords 42 languages and multiple currencies, and can adapt to the changing local laws and mandatory requirements in 37 countries and territories.

Dynamics 365 Finance is a foundation of business operation optimization, risk mitigation, and complete flexibility, such as infinite financial dimension and fraud protection capabilities tied together with real-time reporting and KPIs. Dynamics 365 Finance can take your finance team to a modernized state. It has the functionality and capability to grow with the organization from a feature or cost perspective, including reduced time and cost. It approaches finance in three stages:

1. **Foundation:** Foundational accounting in finance creates a base with general ledger, accounts payable, accounts receivable, project accounting, budgeting, and fixed asset capabilities.
2. **Expand:** As an organization expands or consolidates, the credit management, contract management, and revenue recognition capabilities of Dynamics 365 Finance help companies to drive growth.
3. **Modernize:** Dynamics 365 Finance helps companies to form a modernized finance and accounts team to meet business goals through AI-driven predictive analytics; intelligent, actionable insights with electronic invoicing; other enterprise application integration; and a Power Platform integration.

The following sections discuss some modules that are covered in Dynamics 365 Finance.

Accounts Payable

Accounts Payable is a liability account that shows how much a business owes to its supplier's product and services that it bought or received on credit. Some capabilities of Dynamics 365 Finance's Accounts Payable module are:

- With the help of the Accounts Payable module, organizations can efficiently and effectively manage liabilities.
- It helps in distributing taxes, expenses, and charges across the accounts.
- It helps manage your vendors, purchase orders, transactions, discounts, and invoices to reduce liability and generate more significant income.

Here are some ways that Accounts Payable can be managed in an organization using Dynamics 365 Finance:

1. **Order product or service.** To order products and services for an organization, you need to create purchase requisitions.
   a. **Purchase requisition.** A purchase requisition is a document that allows the purchasing department to buy products or services. Once it gets approved, you can use it to generate a purchase order. To create a purchase requisition, go to the My purchase requisitions page and search and choose the items from a procurement catalog. If the product your organization needs is not in the catalog, you can request that item by entering the product details under the procurement category.
   b. **Purchase order.** It is an external document created by the purchasing department with the list of items and services required by the organization and is submitted to vendors.
2. **Booking payables.** To book payables, the system offers a few options such as invoice registers, invoice journals, vendor invoices, and general journals. All these options are considered as source documents. When any of the source documents is posted, the system records them in ledger or vendor transactions. Vendor transactions can also be considered as module

transactions, and based on these module transactions, the system generates ledger entries.

3. **Due date calculation.** Due date is the date before which a company should pay the liability. The due date is considered a crucial means for accounts payable professionals as it helps them to plan and execute payments. The system offers various options to calculate a due date based on the stipulated settings.

   a. **Terms of payment.** To calculate a due date, the system uses the Invoice Date field and collects all the necessary information from the Terms of payment document. After this, if required, you can also make changes manually in the calculated due date. Payment method is the critical field on the Terms of payment page. This field helps in the calculation of the due date of the invoice. There are two fields, Months and Days, to define the number of days or months added to the due date.

   b. **Payment days.** The system facilitates you to specify payment days for your company. This setting increases the precision of the calculation of the due date. If you define the due date as *not* a Payment date, the system will change it to the next date. For example, if the system's calculated due date is February 14th and your company's specified payment dates are February 13th and February 15th, the system changes the payment date to February 15th automatically.

   c. **Payment calendar.** Unlike payment days, the payment calendar does not specify the payment date. It contains information regarding non-business days when bank services cannot process payments.

   d. **Calculation of due date in invoice general.** The due date is calculated in a journal line. The system uses values of invoice date and the terms of payment to calculate the due date. It also considers payment days and payment calendar.

4. **Payment schedule.** This functionality of the system enables you to schedule your payments if the invoice amount is paid in

a few installments. For this to happen, you need to set up the payment schedule and link it with the terms of the payment document. To access the system's Payment schedule functionality, go to Accounts Payable > Payment setup > Payment schedules. The linked payment schedule is also received by vendors when they select Terms of payment. The vendor is redirected to the Payment schedule page by clicking the payment schedule link. This page shows the schedule for the invoice. It shows the exact dates with amounts that need to be paid. This functionality does not work for invoice journals and registers.

5. **Vendor transactions.** To see vendor transactions, go to Accounts payable > Vendors > All vendors. The system creates vendor transactions when any source document is posted. These transactions can also be referred to as module transactions. You will find the following fields on the vendor transaction page:

   a. **Voucher.** Is a link to vendor and ledger transactions.

   b. **Date.** Represents the date when the operation is accounted for.

   c. **Invoice.** This field is empty for payment transactions. This field also contains the number of invoices linked to the transaction.

   d. **Amount.** The amount of the transaction in the currency of the legal entity.

   e. **Balance.** This field indicates the open balance of the transaction. Suppose the field value is zero; this means that the invoice is settled with a payment. To see all the open transactions, go to Accounts payable > Invoices > Open vendor invoices.

6. **Ledger entries.** Based on the vendor transactions, the system posts ledger transactions. Ledger and vendor transactions are linked via a voucher. Go to the vendor transactions page and click on the Voucher button to open all the ledger transactions.

7. **Pre-pay for the product or service.** Due to the nature of certain goods and services, companies need to make prepayments to their suppliers. These companies use modern software to manage their advance payments. Dynamics 365 Finance

provides two options as a functionality concerning prepayments (advance payments).

a. **Prepayment journal vouchers.** Prepayment using this method is very simple.

    i. Go to the Account payable section.

    ii. Click on the Payments option.

    iii. Shift the slider of the Prepayment Journal Voucher toward the right. While creating a payment, you need to activate this parameter for prepayments. The system will then automatically update the posting profile and set the value that is required for prepayments.

    iv. You can use payment journal vouchers if the payment amount includes sales tax.

b. **Prepayment invoices.** This is another system to manage prepayments. It is available only if you use purchase orders.

    i. **Register a prepayment.** Register a prepayment amount for the purchase order first before creating a prepayment invoice.

    ii. **Create a prepayment invoice.** Open Prepayment Page and go to Accounts payable > Purchase orders > Open prepayments menu item; click the option New prepayment invoice button.

    iii. When you post a prepayment invoice, the system creates a voucher, recorded as a liability in vendor transactions.

    iv. The system uses settings in the accounts payable parameters to specify which profile must be linked to the prepayment invoice.

    v. Once the prepayment invoice is created, the system links the profile with it.

    vi. Now to pay a prepayment invoice, you can use payment proposals.

Now that we have understood some essential functions of the Accounts Payables module in Dynamics 365 Finance, let us see how this system automates vendor invoices processes.

Vendor invoices are like a request or a bill produced to initiate the payment process for provided ongoing services and for specific items and services. It is generated when a purchase order placed with a vendor for services or products is fulfilled. The vendor invoice comprises a header and one or multiple lines for products and services. A vendor invoice can be created with the following steps:

1. If your purchase orders are confirmed, you can use Open vendor invoices and Pending vendor invoices pages to create Vendor Invoice.
2. Use invoice register to enter invoices that are not in reference to any specific purchase order so that you can accrue the expense. Later you can use the vendor invoice approval journal to post them to the vendor balance to reverse the accrual.

Once created, vendor invoices must go through a review process wherein the invoice header, the invoice line, or both are reviewed. Some scenarios can prevent your vendor invoice from being submitted to a workflow:

Scenario 1: When the registered invoice total value and invoice total value is different. There is a feature on the Feature Management page that enables you to obstruct vendor invoice submission to the workflow if the values of the invoice total and registered invoice total are different. Just set the feature on, and it will send an alert to the person who submitted the invoice. This feature helps you to correct balances before resubmitting the invoice to the workflow.

Scenario 2: If the vendor invoice contains unallocated charges. Suppose your vendor invoice is suspected of having unallocated charges, and the parameter that checks it is on the Feature Management page. In this situation, an alert is sent to a person who submitted the invoice to correct it before resubmitting.

Scenario 3: If the vendor invoice you submitted doesn't have a unique invoice number. There is a parameter on the Feature Management page that checks for the duplicate invoice number. If you turn it on, you will receive an alert that the invoice number is not unique so that you can correct it before resubmitting it.
Now let's talk about how you can automate some accounts payable vendor invoices processes.

Automating vendor invoices processes means turning on some advanced features in the Feature Management page. These features are not applicable for invoices that are processed using the Invoice Journal or Invoice Register Journal page. The following are the processes that can be automated:

- **Allowing the system to submit imported vendor invoices to the workflow system automatically.** This capability of the system requires that your process begin with an imported invoice. Invoices that comprise the non-purchase order acquisition category and non-stocked lines or are related to purchase orders can be automatically submitted to the workflow system. You can specify the time-frequency in which you want this process to run in the background. To make the process go smoothly without any manual intervention, you must include an automating posting task in the workflow configuration. If you create invoices manually or via the vendor collaboration invoicing workspace, they can only be submitted manually to the workflow system. This feature also enables you to define company-specific rules for the submission of imported vendor invoices to the workflow system.
- **Automatically matching posted product receipts to invoice lines.** This process uses the defined three-way matching policy, which states the following:
  - The price information on the invoice should be matched with the price information mentioned on the purchase order.

- ■ The quantity information on the invoice should be matched with the quantity information of selected product receipts. This process will also run in the background in a specified time frequency. The process will automatically run until the values of the matched product receipt quantity and the invoice quantity are equal. You also have an option to define the maximum number of times you want the system to try and match product receipts to an invoice line before concluding the process failed. This process can also be run as a stand-alone process.

- ■ Validate the vendor invoice posting before posting it. This feature runs the same validations that are run during the vendor invoice posting. The only difference is, it does not update accounts. This feature saves a lot of time by assuring the invoice's certainty before it is sent for approval.

- ■ Automatic submission of an imported invoice leads to automatic generation of historical information of vendor invoices. This feature enables you to access vendor invoice workflow history directly through the vendor invoice. The automation vendor invoice history contains current steps as well as completed steps. If a step has a glitch or is paused before successful completion, this historical information can help you understand what went wrong in the process and without wasting time, you can rectify the error.

- ■ Automation of vendor invoice analytics and metrics. The Vendor invoices that did not make it through the automated process are found in the vendor invoice entry workspace. It contains tiles that show information about why the invoices failed to reach the workflow system. In this case, accounts payable managers can seek insights from Power BI metrics into the effectiveness of vendor invoice automation.

- ■ Automatically resumes processing of multiple invoices. During automatic processing of multiple invoices, if any invoice is not successfully submitted to the workflow, then in this case, the system will remove that invoice from further automated processing. This way, you get the chance to rectify the issue with the invoice and resubmit it to the workflow. You can go to the Resume automated invoice processing page to restart the automatic processing.

Now that you know how to automate vendor invoicing, we can move on to the next automation process, which is the automation of vendor payment proposals.

Automation of Vendor Payment Proposals

Organizations often need to pay their vendors for purchased products and services. Using the accounts payable system, you can automate the process of creating vendor payment proposals. It empowers you to define a set of rules that can be applied to pay the vendors. For example, you can define which vendors are most important, what amounts should be paid to them, and when they should be paid. Automation of vendor payment proposals enables you to include the following details:

- When to run the payment proposals.
- Defining the criteria to select the invoices that should be paid.
- The resulting journal should be stored in which vendor payment journal.

To access automation for vendor payment proposals, follow these steps:

1. Go to Accounts payable > Payment setup > Process automation.
2. Select Create new process option under Process automation.
3. Then choose the Vendor payment proposal option.
4. Go to the General Page section of the wizard and enter the name of your vendor payment proposal.

5. Now define the person responsible for the payment journal as the owner of the payment journal.
6. The rest of the page settings are generic and define the occurrence pattern for this specific version of the vendor payment proposal.

This wizard does not allow you to define the details of vendor payment proposals, such as when to generate vendor payments, when to print them, or when to post them. Now move to the next page of the wizard, and that is the Vendor Payment proposal page. You can define the criteria for selecting the vendor invoices that need to be paid through this page. These options are also found in the payment proposal in the vendor payment journal, with few exceptions.

To see the occurrence of each payment, go to the process automation weekly view. It has also been added to the Process automation page and Vendor payments workspace. The following are the statuses used to define occurrences:

■ **Scheduled.** This status implies that the payment proposal is scheduled, but it has not yet run.
■ **Error.** This status implies that an error had occurred when the payment proposal ran. To see the errors, click on the View results button.
■ **Completed.** This status implies the successful completion of the payment proposal. To see the payments, click on the View payments link. It opens the payment journal that was created by the occurrence.

You can view the payment amounts in transaction currencies in the journal. You can delete the payment journal using process automation. After you delete a payment, the invoices will be opened for payment. The process automation framework also enables you to edit the payment, the occurrences, and the series created for the payment proposal. If you want to edit the series, either use the process automation page or use the process automation weekly view. While editing a series, the system will prompt you to specify whether you want to make a change to all the occurrences or only to new occurrences.

Accounts Receivable

Many businesses sell their goods and services to customers on credit and then receive the payments a few weeks later. So, businesses need to keep track of the money their customers owe them by using an account in their books called Accounts Receivable.

There are some factors that make the accounts receivable process inefficient, such as:

- Manual processes involving sending reminders and invoices in emails. Processing payments manually might cause customers some inconvenience. If it is difficult for your customers to make the payment manually, they will obviously delay the payment and increase day sales outstanding.
- If your payment system is not connected to the accounting system, it causes double-entry work because it means you have to enter all the details again in your accounting system. This increases the chances of typos and is also very time consuming.
- You might be exposing your customers and their credit card data to the risk of fraud.

To make their payments challenge- and risk-free, you need to automate these processes. Accounts Receivable empowers you to keep track of customer invoices and payments that you receive from customers. This system allows you to set up posting profiles, customer groups, interest notes, commissions, collection letters, and so on. All this information can directly affect transactions of accounts receivable.

If you do not have an automated system and you manually process everything, it is what the process looks like. You have invoices in your accounting system; you email those invoices to your customers or send them through paper mail. Here you are sending a reminder to your customers regarding their outstanding bill. This process contains a lot of issues and is very lengthy. Also, there can always be an issue of mail lost in transit. Your customers can say that they did not receive the invoices. Businesses who usually handle the process manually might have a dedicated collection team to be in contact with customers to collect the payment constantly.

So, instead, you can use the Dynamics 365 Finance Accounts Receivable system to automate this process. It has a collection automation process that can set up collection strategies to automatically classify the customers through invoices that need to be sent a customized email reminder, a programmed process that sends them a collection letter, and collection activity (such as a phone call).

Collection Process Setup Page

Go to Credit and collections > Setup > Collection's process setup.

This page gives you the ability to create an automated collection process that can send email messages, create and post collection letters, and schedule activities. The collection process you create either uses the leading invoice or the oldest open invoice to determine what kind of communication activity should occur with each specific customer.

You can use the customer pool to assign a process hierarchy. Customer Pool can be defined as a group of customers that can be managed for collection processes. You can assign only one hierarchy to each customer pool. But customers can be involved in more than one pool, so, in this case, hierarchy rank will be used to determine the precedence of the process. You can also exclude customers from the automation processes by selecting the option Yes in Exclude from the process field. You also need to enter the amount value, which will be used as a base to compare an invoice or account balance. If the invoice balance is less than the amount value you have set, then that specific customer will automatically be removed from the process.

Credit and Collection Module

The process of recovering the owed amount from customers is not an easy task for organizations. Organizations provide goods and services on credit to potential customers who do not have liquid funds to build a good business relationship. But it would be brilliant if these organizations can forecast which customers will pay on time and which will not to set policies first to avoid any discrepancies later. Dynamics 365 Finance insights can help you to predict customer payment predictions.

Cash collection is usually a reactive process, but the new release wave of Dynamics 365 Finance Insights enables you to apply AI on a customer's historical data to develop a prediction model to know when customers will pay their invoices. To set this up, start with the customer payment setup screen:

1. Go to System administration > Workspaces > Feature management.
2. Find the feature that is named Customer payment insights.
3. Select Enable now.

You have now turned on the Customer payment insights feature; it's ready to be configured.

Now you will get the options to set parameters like which data fields to use and how far you want to go in developing the predictions.

Go to Credit and collections > Setup > Finance insights > Finance insights parameters.

To view the default list of fields used to create the artificial intelligence (AI) prediction model, go to the Financial Insights parameters page and click the Customer payment insights tab. To view data fields, select the View the data fields used in the prediction model link.

If you want to use the default set of fields to build your prediction model, set the Enable feature option to yes on the Financial insights parameters page.

You can now specify the transaction period for your business. Now select Create a prediction model option.

For every open invoice in your business, the prediction model will predict the payments in three buckets:

- **On-time** – Customers who are predicted to pay their invoices on or before the transaction due date.
- **Late** – Customers who will likely pay their invoices after the due date but before the "very late" transaction period.
- **Very late** – Customers who will likely pay their invoices after the start of the "very late" transaction period.

Once the model is published, you get an accuracy score. Now go to the credit and collections workspace; you will see two new tiles:

1. The first tile is showing the number of customers who are predicted to pay late.
2. The second tile is showing the number of transactions predicted to be paid late.

Thus, with a single click of a button, you can train and publish an AI model that can predict based on your historical data when your customers will pay the invoices without any interaction with the developer.

Finance Insights uses behind the scenes a common architecture we explained before: Dynamics 365 Finance operations, export data in real time in an Azure Data Lake Storage, and AI Builder in a Dataverse/Power Platform environment – sending back results directly in the ERP without any AI/data scientist knowledge. You can also extend it if you want, but it's always a good start to jump in machine learning with finance data: empower every person and every organization on the planet to achieve more

Travel Expense

Every company has a team of employees engaged in client meetings, business travels for business development, and new business acquisition and marketing–related tasks to strengthen relationships with prospects and diverse stakeholders—customers, partners, suppliers, influencers, vendors, and so on. These business travels lead to the largest travel and expense budgets that require management of employees' entire lifecycles, from instating a travel request to multilevel approvals to adherence to corporate travel budget and guidelines to inflation of travel and non-travel expense claims for reimbursement.

Some companies still follow manual, paper-driven, inefficient methods to track all the travel expenses, which make the process less accurate and cumbersome. Also, manual handling of the process can lead to the following glitches:

- Manual data entry errors
- Over-budgeting
- Expense reports not submitted on time
- Inaccurate data
- Difficult to detect fraudulent activities
- Lack of mobility and historical data
- Different expense filing processes across various regions and countries

These glitches can lead to delays in the claims' approval and processing, thus building resentment among the employees. Therefore, Microsoft's team integrated the technologies available to them within the Microsoft Azure stack with Microsoft Dynamics 365 business platform.

How much an employee has spent on travel is the data required to file expenses. This data can be drawn from two primary sources:

1. Receipts
2. Credit card transactions

Since credit card transactions take a couple of days to flow in, the receipt-first approach was suitable to go for automation. Receipts are generated immediately upon a transaction, which makes this the most convenient initial input. All employees must use their mobile camera and take a picture of the receipt and upload it to the system. The system then uses a pre-built capability known as a form recognizer that uses advanced machine learning to accurately extract key values from the receipts. The form recognizer's receipt API identifies and extracts key information on sales receipts, such as the transaction time and date, merchant information, the amounts of taxes, totals, and more, with no training required (see Figure 6.1). The API uses optical character recognition technology to capture data from receipts uploaded in various conditions such as faded, crumpled up, or taken in suboptimal lighting conditions. The input to form recognizer is a document or pdf of images, and the output is a structured

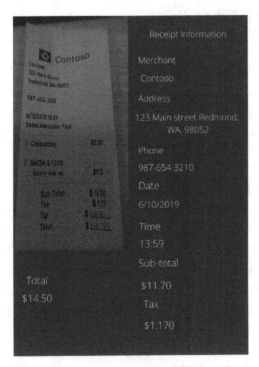

FIGURE 6.1 Automatic receipt recognition.

text, key-value pairs, and tables. It enables you to automate the process of extracting data from your receipts or forms. Using optical character recognition (OCR) and the prebuilt receipt model provided by form recognizer, the receipt API enables these receipt processing scenarios such as business expense reports, tax purposes, reimbursements, budgeting, auditing, marketing, or other purposes. The receipt API also extracts useful data from the receipts such as line items, merchant name, total, tip, and more. There is no need to train your model if you are using this API, you just need to send the receipt image to the analyze receipt API, and the data is extracted. Now you must call the Get Analyze Receipt Result operation. It takes Result ID as input, which was created by the analyze receipt API. The Get Analyze Receipt Result operation returns JSON as an output. The JSON can contain four possible values of status:

1. **Not started.** It means the analysis operation has not yet started.
2. **Running.** It means that the analysis operation is in progress.
3. **Failed.** It means that the operation has failed.
4. **Succeeded.** It means that the analysis operation has succeeded.

You need to call this operation iteratively with an interval of three to five seconds until it returns with the succeeded value. If the status has returned the succeeded value, then the JSON response comprises the receipt understanding and text recognition results. The receipt understanding result is arranged as a dictionary of named field values, where each value contains the normalized value, the extracted text, bounding box, confidence, and corresponding word elements. The text recognition result is organized as a hierarchy of lines and words, with text, bounding box, and confidence information.

Form recognizer is comprised of three parts:

1. **Layout.** It extracts text and tables from your document. It is an official model available as a managed service. To extract text and tables, all you need to do is send your document to the layout

API, and it will extract the text and table and output a structured JSON.

2. **Custom.** Tailored to your form or receipt; extracts text, tables, and key-value pairs. You can use this option to train models specific to your forms data. Here you have two options:

   a. **Train without labels.** This option includes two steps:

      i. **Train.** When you train without labels, human labeling is not required. It is especially used when you have various forms, and you want to train a model for all these types of forms quickly. To train models without labels, you need a handful of sample documents.

      ii. **Analyze.** After training, you can analyze the documents.

   b. **Train with labels.** In this option, you first provide human inputs to extract the values you need and then you label the forms. Again, a handful of sample documents are required to train a model. It enables you to create a continuous feedback loop by adding additional forms to improve the model's accuracy over time.

3. **Pre-built models.** Pre-built models by Microsoft to automate data processing of unique form types; Form recognizer provides pre-built models such as the pre-built receipt model, pre-built business cards model, and pre-built invoice model. We have already discussed the prebuilt receipt model in this section.

These APIs and pre-built models take the assent burden off employees. The complex expense report that would have taken at least 40 minutes of an employee's time can now be completed in a few minutes.

Fraud Detection

In this digitally transformed era, most businesses are moving online to connect with the modern audience and get a higher turnover in a short period of time. But unfortunately, these businesses are also the ones facing the greatest fraud threats. In fact, e-commerce and online merchants lose \$22.8 billion a year due to fraudulent returns and discounts abuse alone. For these businesses to reach their full potential and protect their revenue, they must integrate fraud prevention initiatives.

Microsoft Dynamics 365 Fraud Protection helps merchants protect their revenues and reputations by reducing fraud and abuse and operational expenses, and increasing acceptance rates. Let us look into Microsoft Dynamics 365 Fraud Protection capabilities.

Purchase Protection

Dynamics 365 Fraud Protection with purchase protection capability is a cloud-based solution designed to help e-commerce merchants to protect online revenue by improving online transaction acceptance rates and reducing checkout friction. You can use Dynamics 365 Fraud Protection to examine your historical data. Then it empowers you with powerful tools like the customizable rules engine, the risk support toolset, and more that you can use to fine-tune your fraud protection decisions, encourage your customers, and execute new strategies based on the insights gained from the Fraud Protection service and Microsoft's fraud protection network.

Diagnose Experience Tool

Diagnose experience tool evaluates your historical data and produces reports that provide relevant risk insights into your business's existing fraud patterns. First, you need to upload files for each of these entities for analysis: purchases, payment instruments, products, and chargebacks. Make sure that your historical data files fulfill the following requirements:

- The files should consist of at least 100,000 transactions, 4,000 chargebacks, and 30 days of data. It is recommended to upload at least three months of data.
- The chargeback data in your files should directly correspond to the purchase data of your files. To obtain the best results, ensure

that there are at least five chargebacks associated with every 100 purchases.

Once you upload your data, select Generate reports. Report generation can take up to 24 hours, depending on your file size. The data diagnostic report generated by Diagnose experience is broken down into detailed visual key metrics and charts. Key metrics are comprised of the chargeback match rate that indicates purchase and chargeback completion and the maximum baseline chargeback basis points for analysis. Additional charts generated by the Diagnose experience highlight any formatting errors, missing dates, unique entities rendered, and the number of days worth of data incorporated in the uploaded files.

Risk Diagnostic Report

It is time to generate a risk diagnostic report, but first your data's key metrics must attain a minimum quality threshold; else, you will be prompted to improve your data and try again, and if your data diagnostic report generates competent results, then you can generate a risk diagnostic report. This would also take up to 24 hours.

Using the risk diagnostic report, you can evaluate the risk factors enabling fraudulent activity and how it is affecting your business. Based on your historical data, Fraud Protection renders interactive charts for the following information:

- **Model performance.** Risk diagnostic report generates a chart that represents receiver operating characteristic curves that enable you to observe the percentage of rejected transactions that have chargebacks versus the percentage of legitimate rejected transactions. You can adjust the graphs by using the risk score slider. The chart helps you to understand your detection and false-positive rates at varying thresholds of acceptable risk.
- **Distribution of transactions by risk score.** It distributes the transactions in such a manner that you can easily observe the

reported ratio of fraudulent to non-fraudulent historical transactions. Depending upon their risk scores, these transactions are plotted. To see the selected ranges in detail, you can zoom in.

■ **Top five risk factors.** The report displays the top risk factors for transactions with the highest risk scores. These factors can help you prevent future fraudulent activities.

After getting a diagnosis report and risk diagnostic report, you can upload your purchase protection data into Evaluate and Protect experience to train your model and enhance its accuracy.

Use Evaluate Experience for Fraud Protection

Dynamics 365 Fraud Protection Evaluate experience enables you to send real-time transactions traffic through real-time APIs to get an accurate evaluation and comparison between existing fraud solutions and fraud protection measures. You can also use it to tune your business model by uploading historical and asynchronous data to tailor your risk management strategies, gain insights, and provide customer support. Features of Evaluate experience include:

■ **Fraud protection network.** Dynamics 365 Fraud Protection uses Microsoft AI platform to estimate the probability of the transaction being fraudulent. It enables you to benefit from connected knowledge to obtain broad awareness of fraud activities across the globe while keeping the security of your confidential information and shoppers' privacy in mind. AI platform analyzes the historical data of fraudulent transactions that resulted in fake card details and events that lead to deceitful activities in the past and then uses this data to train machine learning models and detect fraud linkages across all merchants in the fraud protection network. If you engage with this network, you can get collective insights derived from other merchants' experiences. This way, you can be prepared for the events other merchants have already endured.

■ **Provide customer support.** This feature enables your agents to evaluate, search, and investigate the history of your customers' past transactions with your business and identify and unblock customers whose purchase trials are being mistakenly rejected, and block future purchases from suspicious users.

Use Protect Experience for Fraud Protection

The Protect Experience tool in Microsoft Dynamics 365 Fraud Protection enables Fraud Protection to embed into your full production environment. Implementation of Protect Experience provides model scores that can be used to decide whether to accept or reject transactions, and it also mediates escalations from customers. It also shares pertinent information regarding the transaction's integrity with involved banks and issuers to boost their acceptance rates. It generates a scorecard that reflects the performance of Fraud Protection in real time. However, the Evaluate experience generated scorecard enables you to evaluate Microsoft Dynamics 365 Fraud Protection's capabilities.

You can use the data displayed in these scorecards to gain your business insights and make appropriate risk management decisions. The scorecard reports are comprised of key metrics to understand the monthly performance of your fraud protection system. Key metrics charts displayed in the scorecard reports include:

■ **Transaction volume.** It represents the total count of transactions sent for evaluation.
■ **Final approval rate.** It represents the percentage of purchases that are approved out of the total volume.
■ **Settled rate.** It represents the percentage of bank approvals out of the total volume sent to banks.
■ **Chargeback rate by received date.** It represents the percentage of chargebacks out of the total volume approved by banks depending on the receive date of chargeback and the transaction date.

You can use the Virtual Fraud Analyst to analyze and adjust optimal risk score thresholds. Virtual Fraud Analyst uses artificial intelligence to help you balance the lost revenue relating to the chargebacks, refunds, and fees against the customers. It also provides a compelling view of your historical data that can be used to set up rules that guide you on whether you should accept or reject real-time transactions.

Acceptance Booster Service

All the assessments and purchase insights that you have gained using Dynamics 365 Fraud Protection can be shared with the issuing banks and networks through a feature called acceptance booster service. The acceptance booster service empowers you to share real-time transactional trust knowledge with issuing banks and networks by using a direct communication channel.

Another option to use the acceptance booster service is to receive MID recommendations from Fraud Protection. These recommendations are then incorporated into your authorization requests, leading to a higher overall acceptance rate.

You can use both the options provided by the acceptance booster service on the same transactions where applicable. But it is recommended to use the MID recommendation option for transactions on banks that are not participating in the acceptance booster service.

The adaptive artificial intelligence used by Dynamics 365 Fraud Protection provides merchants with insights that help them to make decisions that balance revenue opportunity and customer experience versus fraud loss. This technology continuously learns from patterns to help increase fraud detection accuracy, which protects your revenue by decreasing wrongful rejections and increasing e-commerce transactions acceptance rates. Dynamics 365 Fraud Protection with purchase protection capability also helps reduce operational expenses by reducing manual review processes. Purchase protection capability helps reduce the challenges and frictions in the shopping experience via the transaction acceptance booster feature, which helps you to provide the smoothest online purchasing experience to your deserving customers.

Account Protection

Dynamics 365 Fraud Protection with account protection is designed to safeguard user accounts from abuse and fraud by resisting fake account creations, account takeover, and fraudulent account access. Fake account creation is ubiquitous today. It is an automated creation of illegitimate accounts that are created to commit malicious activities, and it does not belong to any genuine user. With the evolving attack techniques, it is becoming difficult for businesses to detect fake account attacks and unauthorized account access because more account registrations are an indication of growth. Therefore, they don't investigate these accounts too rigorously.

To effectively detect fake account activities, it has become a necessity to use a fraud detection system. Dynamics 365 Fraud Detection account protection capability uses adaptive artificial intelligence to assess frauds for all the critical steps of account lifecycle, enabling merchants to block fraudulent activities before the damage is caused. It provides multiple layers of defense for each event of account lifecycle:

■ **Preventing fake account creation.** To prevent automated fake account creation and unauthorized access to existing accounts, merchants use a list of compromised credentials and the number of trial-error attempts made by the attacker (brute force) to detect malicious activity. Dynamics 365 account protection uses device fingerprinting based on adaptive artificial intelligence to obtain account and forensics data as the first line of defense. It provides a scorecard that maps to the probability of whether a bot is trying to create an account. It provides API for real-time risk assessment and rules to optimize risk strategy, keeping your business requirements in mind. The scorecard shows the APIs that you can customize. You can select events data by time and view events from the last hour or the last 24 hours. Key metrics indicators shown in the scorecards include:

- **Bot score distribution.** A bot model score is a number between 0 and 999 that shows the probability that the bot is trying to create a new account or sign into an account. A higher score indicates a bot is initiating the event.
- **Top bot countries and regions.** This chart comprises a geographic view of the five countries and regions that shows the percentage of total events initiated from a specific country or region, especially countries with a bot score of above 900.
- **Risk model scores.** This model score can help merchants by indicating the probability of a fraudulent event.
- **Rule decision trend.** This chart shows the percentage of approved, challenged, viewed, or rejected decisions based on the rules defined by you.
- **Real-time assessment of risk.** To generate risk assessment scores, fraud protection uses AI models for account creation and account login events. The score generated by AI models is then taken into consideration by merchants to define rules to protect their business and its reputation.

Dynamics 365 Fraud Detection account creation protection helps you avoid incurring losses, protecting your bottom line. It helps protect your customers against automated attacks, safeguards their user accounts from abuse and fraud, reduces account login friction, keeps your customers' data safe, strengthens your reputation, and improves customer engagement. By implementing the device fingerprinting capability of fraud protection, merchants can boost the acceptance rates. These fraud detection capabilities empower your e-commerce team to help reduce friction from CAPTCHA or two-factor authentication, giving your customers a world-class shopping experience and keeping your business buzzing.

Loss Prevention

Dynamics 365 Fraud Protection with loss prevention capability is intended to detect potential frauds on returns attempted through omni-channel purchases and discounts to help preserve profits. Loss prevention capability empowers store managers to take action to mitigate losses promptly. Let us understand with an example of how the potential frauds occur that results in loss of revenue.

Businesses often sell their products at a discounted price to increase sales. So assume that a customer bought a product from your eCommerce website at a discounted price. Then he goes to your store in the city and returns it, receiving not the discounted price he paid online but the product's actual price without discount. In cases like this, merchants suffer the loss of revenue because of the system's internal failure.

Dynamics 365 fraud protection with loss prevention capability uses artificial intelligence to analyze your historical data and recognize oddities and patterns that might indicate in-store fraud. All you need to do is upload historical data, including transactional data, sales, payments, and payment methods, into the system. The adaptive artificial intelligence models will then search for patterns and anomalies and generate reports that show actionable insights about any anomalies or trends detected by the AI models. Store managers can use these reports with actionable insights to take immediate action on anomalous entities based on the risk scores.

Loss prevention not only protects revenue by reducing loses; it also analyzes omni-channel fraudulent patterns for anomalies and provides merchants with business intelligence reporting to increase the visibility of potentially fraudulent activity of business entities. It makes your omni-channel business run smoothly.

 DEMAND FORECASTING

What is the top challenge faced by businesses today? It is demand volatility. There are too many factors to be taken into consideration that affect buyers, causing them to change their minds frequently. It can be anything from posts by social media influencers to weather inconsistencies that can change a customer's willingness to buy a product. Hence, we need demand forecasting.

Demand forecasting is a business practice performed to optimize inventory workflow. In this process, historical sales data is analyzed to make estimations about customer demands in the future. Demand forecasting helps businesses make critical business assumptions such as turnover, cash flow, profit margins, capital expenditure, and capacity planning. Typical challenges faced by businesses in planning stocks are:

- Meeting sales demand without overstocking.
- Planning promotions.
- Managing abnormal demand.
- Managing new and obsolete products.
- Planning products with irregular demand.

Demand forecasting can help manage stocks better, but you need a forecasting tool that can do more than simply calculate forecast from demand history. It needs to be able to forecast demand increases arising from promotions and manage overlapping promotions and different time periods covered by different promotions.

Dynamics 365's demand forecasting addresses all these issues. It uses historical data to generate a statistical baseline forecast. The historical transactional data is in the supply chain management transactional database. This data is gathered and fed to the machine learning service. With minimal customization, it enables you to plug multiple data sources, such as comma-separated value (CSV) files, Dynamics 365 Finance & Operations, and Microsoft Excel files into the staging table. Hence, it empowers you to generate demand forecasts having historical data spread among multiple systems. However, the master data must be the same across the diverse data sources.

You can use the Demand forecasting machine learning experiments; they are best among forecasting methods to calculate a baseline forecast. To manage the parameters for these forecasting methods, go to Supply Chain Management.

All the changes made to the demand forecasts in early iterations are available in Supply Chain Management, including the forecasts and the historical data.

 CONNECTED STORE

Today, many retail brands are using modern technology such as intelligent data use to run their businesses successfully. In the digital transformation of the retail business, retailers try to gather insights between customers, personnel, operations, and products. At present, for a lot of retailers, this digital feedback loop is broken for their physical channels. There is limited visibility of operations and customers in their stores, leading to a negative impact on operational efficiency and customer experiences that may cause revenue loss. For example, retailers want to know the effectiveness of promotions; they want to know shelf voids. They want to have the intelligence to understand and manage queues. The actual problem is they are not getting enough data from operations and customer activities in their store. A connected store is designed to provide enough data to get insights to resolve all the issues. It generates observational data that can be harnessed and analyzed to make better business decisions.

Dynamics 365 connected store is the application that helps retail businesses to maximize the potential of their observational data. Using this application, you can learn a lot about your store and the shoppers shopping at your store by using video cameras and IoT sensors. Connected store empowers employees with tools that make them more accurate and efficient. Features provided by the Dynamic 365 connected store include:

- **Insights indicating busiest hours of your store.** You can place cameras on entrances and exits and use shoppers analytics skills to study traffic patterns to know the total footfall on your busiest days, like on weekends. It may also help you determine your business's peak hours and which entrance gets the most used. If you have these kinds of insights, you can easily manage your store employees' shifts to run it more effectively.

■ **Notifies when your store hits maximum capacity.** Dynamics 365 connected store also enables you to set up occupancy thresholds based on fire safety and health guidelines. This feature lets you know if your store reaches maximum capacity, allowing you to ensure your visitors' and the staff's safety.

■ **Know which displays of your store are gaining more engagement.** The cameras facing your offers and promotions use display effectiveness skill to learn which displays are getting more engagement from shoppers. If any display is doing well, you can dig in and learn more about shoppers' traffic patterns so that you can optimize the layout of your store.

■ **Assists in the upgrading of customer experience.** With cameras facing the queues, you can use the queue management skill to monitor wait times, making it easier for you to know when to open an additional register or checkout counter to ensure your customers have the best experience.

Dynamics 365 connected store gives a real-time understanding of what is happening in your store. The data collected by cameras and IoT sensors provide not only digital insights but also spatial insights available in their physical environment that can help your staff to be available for customers when they need them.

Today, online retailers can track their customer behavior in many details and then tie it back to their purchase pattern. They can use this data to optimize the customer experience, vis-a-vis the stocks and the sales. However, for retailers that own physical stores, there is still a massive physical divide. Most retailers do not know the right data to track real-world actions, because of which they miss opportunities.

With the connected store, you can bridge this gap between the physical and digital worlds by leveraging real-time observational data through computer vision and IoT sensors and generating perception data to provide intelligent endpoints. Multiple sensing factors are consolidated along with your transactional data into summaries and visualizations and enlighten you with the next best actions or recommendations. By using a connected store, you can complete the digital feedback loop, and you can optimize operations, customer experiences, and product sales. Following are the phases of the loop:

Observation phase. The connected store is where data ingestion happens. We ingest connected stores with camera feeds and get contextual data from space, for example, weather and traffic patterns. We then get transactional data from our POS systems. The connected store then co-relates and analyzes this data from spatial, contextual, and transactional data stores. This contextualization is then provided to you in the form of summaries and visualizations.

Correlation phase. In this phase, you collect data that impact your sales, customer engagement, or foot traffic, for example, if you have displayed two promotions in your store and want to know which promotion is getting more response from your customers and on which day; or if you want to understand the impact of a promotion on the proximity of an entrance. To get this kind of data, you can correlate the pull-through of a promotion based on its location in the store.

Recommendation phase. Based on the correlation, Dynamics 365 connected store provides you recommendations. These recommendations will provide answers to the questions like what to display, where to place it in your store, when to open a new queue, and when you need to staff more employees.

Action phase. Now, you need to perform actions based on the recommendations you got. The connected store can leverage multiple channels to communicate with your workers, and these workers will both be at stores and your head office. So, in terms of communication, you can use custom protocols to leverage power, automate, and team tasks. It also gives you options to send push notifications and send emails, with dashboard summaries using Power BI.

Now let us see who can benefit from the connected store:

- **Associates.** They receive timely alerts with precise instructions to execute the daily tasks efficiently.
- **Store managers.** They know the stores quite well. Connected stores help them with contextual data about their stores. They see store traffic and patterns and have data available to them about queues and wait times. All the contextual data that the store manager receives from one store can be consolidated and understood on a multi-store level. If making a certain change has worked for one store, it might work for all of the store branches.
- **Merchandisers.** They are considered key beneficiaries of connected store applications. They are armed with not only sales data for promotion, but they can also understand pull-throughs and dwell time, engaging displays both in terms of traffic and dwell times.

Using Dynamics 365 connected store, operational patterns that went unrecognized are now translated into insights. It allows your employees to act faster and encourages businesses to run smoothly. Dynamics 365 connected store is a comprehensive solution for retailers to drive operational excellence, empower employees, and provide exceptional customer experiences.

ML FOR HUMAN RESOURCES MANAGEMENT

Employees are the reason for any business to achieve success. If your employees are carefully nurtured, they intend to keep your customers happy to ensure business continuity and growth. Despite this, many modules require a well-organized HR management system, as it is a very tedious and time-consuming task. It is a requisite for every business to manage and employ the available resources and hold on to the most important business assets in the best possible manner.

To fulfill all business elements, businesses are making a smart move of switching to a human resource management system. Dynamics 365 Human Resources management system is a cloud-based solution that helps organizations strategically accomplish, empower, and optimize the resources. It encourages employees to enrich their careers proactively. It guides them to complete the needed training and suggest professional development resources to drive future success.

Microsoft Dynamics 365 Human Resources uses artificial intelligence and machine learning to automate numerous employee-oriented processes and deliver accurate records. It is an effective solution:

- To manage the organizational structures of your business.
- For sustaining information of employees from their hiring to retirement.
- For the recruitment of applicants and their application tracking.
- To generate pay information and track profile-based time management
- To determine and manage benefit plans, designate beneficiaries, enroll workers, and assign dependent coverage.
- To create and observe absence policies.
- For reviewing employees' performances.

Dynamics 365 Human Resources capabilities include:

- **Transform employee experience.**
  - **Employee self-service portal.** You can free up your HR team by giving employees self-service access to Microsoft Dynamics Human Resources directly within Microsoft Teams. For this, they need to install the Human Resources app from Microsoft Teams marketplace. After installation,

employees can easily request leave or time off from wherever they are. With the app installed, employees gain access to the powerful AI chatbot for all their leaves and absence queries. The employees just have to type some keywords related to their query, and the chatbot responds immediately. Even if you want to know your leave balance, it quickly surfaces the amount of time you have left divided by leave type. The leave type includes standard sick and vacation days, including any specific leave program added by the HR team to comply with new government regulations or company offerings. After knowing your leave balances in detail, you can then perform actions from the same team's chat that you are having with the chatbot. You only must enter a specific time off request, and the chatbot will itself create a draft, including a calendar view with start and end dates and your remaining balance. The draft request stays available until you decide on your dates. When you have decided the dates, just go to your saved drafts, make any edits if needed, and submit. Managers can easily review your request and approve employees' requests with just a few clicks. This process saves a lot of time for employees and empowers them with self-service access.

Using self-service portals, employees can also track their performance, manage goal setting, and do certification tracking.

- ■ **Team performance details.** This portal enables managers to analyze the performance of their teams and address any immediate concerns.
- ■ **Hire the right people.** Dynamics 365 Human Resources makes it easy for managers to hire the right people. It integrates seamlessly with LinkedIn so managers can get in touch with qualified candidates and build pipelines. It enables automatic interview scheduling and simplified feedback. It is designed to keep managers in the loop at every stage and helps in making smarter hiring decisions. The application helps drive engagement from employees' first days of work by providing them

personalized onboarding plans that outline important tasks and training, sharing required resources, and helping them make the right connections within your company. Dynamics 365 Human Resources delivers a complete view of employees and their experience by centralizing your HR programs from benefits to conversation and absence reporting.

■ **Optimization of your HR process.** Dynamics 365 Human Resources drives excellence in your HR operations to reduce costs and create a more connected environment for employees.

   ■ **Create flexible compensation plans.** Add all available benefits in the benefits management tool; define eligibility rules according to the benefit. You can set an enrollment period for each benefit. This would enable employees to self-enroll, saving time and effort of HR employees. The data analytics generated in benefits management transforms complex benefits data into easy-to-understand insights, helping managers plan. Interactive visualizations allow managers to instantly filter and see the benefits of the most popular employee plans, which helps to inform strategy.

   ■ **Leave and expense management.** HR employees can use this tool to easily customize employee time off guidelines like flexible dates and approval rates. Using Dynamics 365 Human Resources, you can define leave and absence terms to ensure accurate data entry and tracking.

   ■ **Compensation management.** It is used to set fixed and variable compensation plans and create more tailored plans that better fit your needs like the band, grade, step, and regional plans. You can easily see the number of employees assigned to a particular plan along with the compensation structure. HR employees are empowered by the process engine that automates compensation changes to specific employees. It can also perform bulk changes for a full team or for the entire organization. Embedded analytics help HR employees with a clear picture of their compensation data, enabling them to track and nurture demographic equality across the organization.

- **Discover workforce insights.** Dynamics 365 Human Resources helps you to optimize your organizational structure and automates routine tasks so that HR experts can concentrate more on strategy. The home screen of this application is easy to navigate and is role specific. This ensures that workspaces are secure while providing quick access to detailed information and helping your organization reduce administrative costs.
  - **Personnel management.** HR management employees have their own personnel management workspace and can instantly view crucial employee data and see candidates to hire, new employees starting soon, and the ones retiring or leaving the organization. HR experts can view full employee records and perform actions from here. Employee records are connected to all operational HR process to streamline tasks like employment verification, benefits enrollment, changing roles, and terminating employees. Dynamics 365 Human Resources uses AI to connect data and employees to gain insightful analytics and guidance.
  - **Improve workforce planning.** Both HR and managers find it difficult to navigate through multiple screens to get analytics reports of data in real time held across the various system. Power BI helps you to bring together all your data for analyzing and visualizing it on one device and making appropriate decisions.
  - **Common data service.** Dataverse (formerly known as common data service) are the tables designed to capture common concepts and scenarios within an organization. It securely stores and manages data used by any internal or external business applications.

- **Skill-gap analytics.** This enables you to align workforce skills with specific job skills and business needs.
- **Identify employee sentiments.** Using the customer's voice, companies can record their employees' feedback in real time and analyze their sentiment so that action can be taken on matters that need immediate attention. Microsoft Forms Pro surveys also capture valuable feedback of employees using custom or ready-to-use templates.

MACHINE LEARNING AT THE WORKPLACE

How do businesses measure success? They use pointers such as revenue, customer satisfaction, and time to market, but is it enough to just measure success?

You can drive success by leveraging your most powerful predictor: day-to-day actions performed by people, including their behavior and how they communicate, collaborate, and navigate processes with their team. How they build their network, innovate, and build a relationship with their customers. All this information directly impacts your business outcomes because what separates high-performance organizations from the rest is how people work. If you could quantify and analyze how everyday work impacts your business, you could predict and control your outcomes. By harnessing the data insights with the data you already have, you can identify the patterns that can lead your business to success. This is the kind of information you need to empower your workforce to move forward swiftly, foster innovation, feel happier, and create more value for your customers. Workplace intelligence insights can unlock new potential and predictive capabilities for breakthrough business performance.

Workplace analytics is all about helping employees to perform their jobs more effectively. It is tricky to understand what can make employees more effective. There is very little data to understand which team is performing better than others. Office 365 provides the data that you need to understand problems like why one team delivers better results and on time while others do not.

Office 365 comprises data like all the emails, meetings, chats, documents, and all the other stuff that is just lying around in it. It is known to be the largest dataset ever created that contains information about how people spend their time at work.

What workplace analytics does is harness the data from the employees' everyday work and use that data to gain insights and look for inefficiencies. It enables you to take action to improve overall productivity.

Home. On the home page of Workplace Analytics, you can view the population and the months of data gathered to obtain insights. It is like a dashboard; the page gives you the statistics on the employees' work hours. Let us start with some of the visualizations at the bottom of the page. These visualizations provide a quick insight into what you need:

- **Week in life.** It enables you to pick any team, group, or function and understand what a week in their life looks like, including what hours they spent between meetings and work and how many after-hours they have spent despite workday collaboration hours? The employees are considered active and are included in the data if they have sent even one email or message. Meetings and email hours help you quantify the collaboration volume and patterns within the company. If your employees' excess time is spent on meetings and emails, it becomes stressful for employees. Workplace Analytics helps analytics to identify high and low collaboration and its causes. If a lot of time is spent on low-quality meetings, a company can take action against it.
- **Meetings overview.** In this visualization, you can see meeting norms set by your organization. Here you can view metrics about specific meeting components to determine insights by analyzing the meeting's quality, such as duration, number of attendees, redundancy, multitasking, and conflicting meeting

hours. This is done to make meetings more efficient. It also helps to recognize if meeting attendees were multitasking like sending emails during the meeting, which means the attendees were not contributing their full potential in the meeting. This is the kind of information you need to improve the productivity of employees.

▪ **Management and coaching.** This visualization contains information regarding collaboration between managers, teams, employees, and leaders. The analyst of your company can use this information to understand the relationship between employees and their managers. The metrics in this visualization enable the analyst to classify a group of under- or over-coached employees. The time with manager histogram shows metrics of employees' time spent on meetings with their managers each week. Insights gained from this visualization can help you spot newly onboarded employees who are not getting sufficient guidance from their managers. Further, you can compare the time of manager and employee tenure, employee satisfaction, and the job role to gain insights regarding opportunities for improvement.

▪ **Networks and collaboration.** This visualization shows network connections between various teams within the company. Network size and network breadth help you understand whether the employees of a particular team are working in an insular way or connected with multiple people.

▪ **Microsoft Viva insights.** It is an app in Microsoft Teams that helps people by collaborating communications, learning, resources, knowledge, and insights to enhance employee experiences by integrating seamlessly into the apps you use every day. Types of Viva insights are:

 ▪ **Personal insight.** Only you can see your personal insights. It is derived from the data gathered through your emails, calls, chats, and meetings. Based on these insights, you get useful recommendations on how you can utilize your time more effectively, such as when to take a break and when to focus on work and learning that can help you boost productivity on what you do.

▪ **Team insights.** You can see manager insights here. It showcases patterns like meeting overload, minimum focus time, and after-hours meetings that can lead to burnout and stress. Managers can use these insights and take actions to balance the well-being of employees and their productivity.

▪ **Organizational insights.** Organizational insights are for business leaders to understand the impact of work on their people and business. They can act on matters to prevent organizational resiliency and can see opportunities where a change in process could improve business outcomes.

To perform a detailed analysis, you can use the Power BI Connector to combine Power BI and Workplace Analytics data to use drill-down and visualization capabilities of Power BI. Power BI automatically refreshes your data with new data from Workplace Analytics. The connector also strengthens privacy by limiting those who view the report from seeing data about a group specified by the Workplace Analytics administrator. This gives you the confidence to share reports without worrying about the data being exposed.

MyAnalytics Dashboard

MyAnalytics Dashboard provides insights to employees to help them understand how they can better manage their time and work more efficiently. The dashboard gives a detailed visualization of how much time you have spent on collaboration, network, focused work, and well-being. It also suggests some productivity insights, educational tips, time spent on meetings, and how an individual can improve productivity.

If you combine MyAnalytics and Workplace Analytics using Workplace Analytics plans, the insights gained can generate an improvement plan to help team members increase focus time and reduce meeting load while maintaining their work-life balance, among other goals.

Afterword

I T IS GREAT TO eventually see a book focused on machine learning (ML) and artificial intelligence (AI), specifically for Power Platform and Dynamics. Frankly, I am surprised that no one came up with it sooner. Aurélien and Vinnie, realizing the importance of the subject and seeing the nonexistence of any other book on this topic, have put together an amazing book for Microsoft Dynamics 365 and Power Platform developers, solution architects, and technical consultants.

Machine learning and artificial intelligence technologies are coming out of the hype cycle and are now a core part of many organizations' digital transformation strategies. Organizations want to leverage the technologies to reduce operational costs, generate customer insights, and build and improve customer experiences. These technologies are helping organizations to automate, simplify, and accelerate their processes and operations to improve both employee and external customer experiences. Along with improved operational efficiencies, ML and AI are enabling companies to create products and services that lead to changes in their business models with huge potential for revenue growth.

Top software and cloud providers like Microsoft are providing ML and AI tools and services to their customers to democratize ML and AI, thus helping organizations accelerate in realizing their business use cases by utilizing these emerging technologies.

Since Power Platform and Dynamics 365 applications are built on top of Microsoft's Azure Cloud platform, it is very easy for developers and technical architects to utilize tools such as Azure Machine

Learning designer, Azure AutoML, Azure Notebooks, or AI Builder. AI Builder is offered specifically for Power Platform and Dynamics 365. AI Builder comes with many prebuilt ML models for common business use cases and can be utilized with a simple point and click without any coding experience.

No matter what industry you belong to, AI Builder can help you in enabling common or special business use cases. AI Builder is available in Power Platform (Power Apps, Power Automate, and Power Virtual Agents). It comes bundled with common ML models such as category classification, business card reader, receipt processing, text translation, sentiment analysis, and many more.

A savvy business power user or a citizen developer can use AI Builder and any of the prebuilt ML models to quickly build an AI application in the Power Platform and Dynamics 365. However, professional developers can also utilize AI Builder to build, train, and deploy custom models that an organization may want to include in their Power Platform and Dynamics 365 AI applications. The book has done a good job in exploring and discussing Azure Machine Learning services and AI Builder and how to quickly utilize the machine learning models with Power Platform and Dynamics 365.

Azure Machine Learning service and AI Builder are just the beginning of tools and services that are going to continue to grow in scope and help in commoditizing machine learning and AI with developers and technical architects for building and enhancing business applications.

This book is going to be a perfect guide for Power Platform and Dynamics 365 developers and technical architects to quickly get started with machine learning and start building intelligent applications for their business use cases.

Fawad Khan, Microsoft

Index